"Gupta's *Galatians* offers ⬚⬚⬚⬚⬚⬚⬚⬚⬚⬚⬚⬚⬚ e survey of the epistle's conten⬚⬚⬚⬚⬚⬚⬚⬚⬚⬚⬚ theological themes. His compelling argument that the letter's leitmotif is the theme of kinship or family sheds new light on familiar theological discussions, including justification by faith and participation in Christ."

—*Lynn Cohick,* distinguished professor of
New Testament, Houston Christian University

"Gupta not only introduces readers to Galatians and to recent Pauline scholarship bearing upon its interpretation, but he also flags and reflects upon three leading epistolary themes, namely, family, faith, and freedom. If you are looking for a scholarly point of entry into this celebrated and complicated Pauline letter, then look no further."

—*Todd D. Still,* Charles J. and Eleanor McLerran
DeLancey Dean & William M. Hinson Professor
of Christian Scriptures, Baylor University

"Readers are treated here with a reliable guide to what makes Galatians tick—its literary structure, history of scholarship, and the heart of Paul's gospel as it pertains to themes such as family, faith, and freedom."

—*Joshua Jipp,* professor of New Testament,
Trinity Evangelical Divinity School

"Well-written, clear, insightful, and theologically rich, Gupta's *Galatians* is a fine guide to the heart of Paul's gospel logic in this early Christian letter. This volume will be a valuable resource for preaching, teaching, and worship in the church."

—*Darian Lockett,* professor of New Testament,
Talbot School of Theology, Biola University

"In *Galatians*, Nijay Gupta offers an informative and engaging guide for understanding the crucial theological themes in Paul's letter. Readers will appreciate his brief overview of the background and content of the letter and clear explanations of the major scholarly conversations concerning the letter's theology."

—*Janette H. Ok,* associate professor of
biblical studies, Fuller Seminary

"In this inaugural New Word Biblical Themes volume, Nijay Gupta sets a high standard for the rest of the series. His clarity, sound judgment, and ability to help readers wrestle with and through these texts reflect a reverence borne of Christian identity and a level of knowledge manifesting the best of the academic enterprise."

—*David B. Capes,* director, Lanier Theological Library

"Gupta's volume welcomes us to what he dubs the 'theological buffet of Galatians' and invites readers to sit down at the table and take part in an ongoing conversation. In doing so, he provides an ample menu, so to speak, in both topics and further reading lists, that promises to nourish discussions in classrooms and beyond."

—*Kara Lyons-Pardue,* professor of New Testament,
Point Loma Nazarene University

"Nijay Gupta explores the many themes in Galatians around the poles of family, faith, and freedom. The result is a helpful introduction to many tricky topics including justification by faith, the law, circumcision and covenant, the fruit of the Spirit, gospel and law, and more."

—*Michael F. Bird,* lecturer in theology, Ridley College

9

WORD BIBLICAL THEMES NEW

GALATIANS

NIJAY K. GUPTA

ZONDERVAN
ACADEMIC

ZONDERVAN ACADEMIC

Galatians
Copyright © 2024 by Nijay K. Gupta

Published in Grand Rapids, Michigan, by Zondervan. Zondervan is a registered trademark of The Zondervan Corporation, L.L.C., a wholly owned subsidiary of HarperCollins Christian Publishing, Inc.

Requests for information should be addressed to customercare@harpercollins.com.

Zondervan titles may be purchased in bulk for educational, business, fundraising, or sales promotional use. For information, please email SpecialMarkets@Zondervan.com.

ISBN 978-0-310-12720-8 (softcover)
ISBN 978-0-310-12721-5 (ebook)

Cover design: Tammy Johnson
Interior typesetting: Kait Lamphere

Printed in the United States of America
24 25 26 27 28 LBC 5 4 3 2 1

Contents

EDITORIAL BOARD

CONTRIBUTORS

Series Preface

In 1982, F. F. Bruce's 1–2 Thessalonians commentary was among the first volumes to appear in the now highly esteemed Word Biblical Commentary series (1982–). A handful of years later, the Word Biblical Themes series began publication with Leslie Allen's Psalms and Ralph Martin's Philippians volumes, both printed in 1987. The WBT series was designed to supplement the WBC by offering short discussions of the most important themes in each biblical book. While the WBC volumes were technical and lengthy, focusing on an audience of scholars, the WBT series was meant to distill the key messages of biblical texts to help students and pastors as they present Scripture's testimony to form churches today.

Over the last forty-five years the Word Biblical Commentary series has almost reached completion of its fifty-two volumes, and some older volumes have been revised. However, the original Word Biblical Themes series only managed to produce fifteen volumes between 1987–1991. Therefore, we are pleased to now carry on the original vision of this supplement series with *New* Word Biblical Themes, allowing a new generation of scholars to explore the most crucial theological themes in each book of Scripture. These concise guides will inform and enhance Bible study, Christian teaching, and faithful preaching of the Word of God.

The New Word Biblical Themes offers the following features:

- Reliable research from a diverse group of expert scholars
- An up-to-date academic summary of basic issues of background, structure, and content for each biblical book
- Focused study of each biblical book, discussing the most important theological themes
- Insight into the "big picture" of a book of the Bible by understanding what topics and concerns were most important to the biblical writers
- Thoughtful reflection on theological and moral issues facing the church today by showing readers how the biblical writers approached similar issues in their day
- Reading recommendations for those who want to explore topics in more depth

We hope that readers will be blessed by the expertise of the series contributors, enlightened by concise and clear thematic discussions, challenged by fresh ideas and approaches, and encouraged in their own reading of the Bible as a text full of wisdom.

Nijay K. Gupta

Author's Preface

A few years ago, I was working on some research on the New Testament and I needed to explore themes in a particular book. I knew that the Word Biblical Commentary series had a themes supplement series, so I went looking for a volume on the text I was researching. I came to realize that only a handful of books had been produced on New Testament texts for that Word Biblical Themes series—it had never been completed. A group of volumes appeared in the late 1980s and early 1990s, but after that the series went dormant. I then reached out to Katya Covrett, my editor friend at Zondervan and a longtime collaborator in publishing, with the idea of relaunching the whole series: *New* Word Biblical Themes. She and her team were enthusiastically supportive of this idea. The "Word Biblical" name has long been known for high-quality scholarship. And short books covering key themes offer a needed resource to students, scholars, and pastors alike. Galatians was a natural choice for my own volume, since I had recently completed my manuscript on Galatians for Zondervan's Story of God Bible Commentary. This themes volume is not a repeat; I didn't do any "cutting and pasting" from my commentary. This is a fresh book, and I hope it is a contribution in its own right. But, of course, I didn't need to start from scratch on research. It was a labor of love and joy to think on the broadest level, after already writing a commentary, about Paul's enduring messages through a selection of themes. I wrestled with how many themes to choose and about whether or not I chose the right ones. What gave me comfort in the end is my conviction that scholarship is not the last word on a topic; I also believe good research and writing informs others and generates reflection, discussion, and new understanding. I hope that is the case with this book, and for every other volume in this series.

CHAPTER 1

Introduction[1]

[H]ere is Christianity's first great theologian—arguably its greatest theologian—in full flood. Here we can never lose sense that issues of profound significance are in the balance, to be argued for and defended as though life itself was at stake—as, for Paul, it was.

—*James D. G. Dunn*[2]

Paul's letter to the Galatians offers us a glimpse of "raw Paulinism." Nowhere else in the corpus of his letters do we find him so challenged, and perhaps so challenging . . . If there is a single letter that most defines Paul, Galatians is an obvious contender for that title.

—*Bruce Longenecker and Todd D. Still*[3]

Galatians is a text that gets right to the heart of Paul's understanding of the gospel of Jesus Christ. The six chapters of this ancient letter drip with Paul's passion as he pleads with a community he cares about to reject false gospels and maintain the course of true faith. Some scholars

---

1. All Scripture citations in this volume are from Galatians unless otherwise indicated.

2. James D. G. Dunn, *The Theology of Paul's Letter to the Galatians*, New Testament Theology (Cambridge: Cambridge University Press, 1993), xiii.

3. Bruce Longenecker and Todd D. Still, *Thinking through Paul: An Introduction to His Life, Letters, and Theology* (Grand Rapids: Zondervan, 2014), 104.

have remarked that Galatians has the feel of an impulsive and hasty response. But we must not mistake naked honesty for thoughtless reaction. Galatians is a brilliantly well-crafted argument for a new way of knowing God through a dynamic relationship with Jesus, not mediated by works of the (Jewish) Law. We might not be wrestling in the church today with the same exact questions or specific problems that Paul was addressing when he wrote to the Galatian Christians. However, what keeps this letter at the forefront of conversations about New Testament theology is how it touches upon the foundations of Christian faith in such a way that we come to understand what life is all about with and before God—faith, love, mortification of the flesh, goodness in communal life, Spirit-led wisdom, spiritual sensitivity to God's gospel ways from Abraham's day to Paul's. All these virtues have the crucified Christ as their vivifying center. In this book we will explore the thematic colors that comprise Paul's masterful word-art, which we call Galatians. Perhaps you have heard that "justification by faith" is the center of this letter. That's not quite correct, and the unspoken agent—Christ himself—ought to be spoken ("justification *in Christ* by faith"). But there is much more in Galatians than justification, making this epistle a multifaceted three-dimensional model of Paul's conception of Christian faith and life. Equally important to this letter are matters of family, freedom, and formation (and more besides). But, first, we need to get a basic grasp of the context and situation behind the letter.

THE SITUATION

As best we can understand from the incidental pieces of information we have from the New Testament, Paul first came to Galatia (Asia Minor, modern-day Turkey) under dire circumstances. In 4:13 he mentions how a "weakness" (CSB; NRSV: "physical infirmity") was somehow involved in his encounter with them. Perhaps he needed medical treatment and found himself in Galatia, where some in the community had compassion on him and took him in for care. Another theory, which I find more attractive, is that a beaten and bruised Paul was fleeing from persecutors and ended up in Galatia in need of convalescent care.[4] His "weakness," then, wasn't migraines or myopia, but the "thorn in the flesh" of his enemies hunting him down and causing him harm. Whatever the exact case, Paul ended up in Galatia and certain people there welcomed him and showed him hospitality and care (4:14). They shared their strength and resources with Paul, he shared the gospel of Christ with them, and the rest is history. What a pretty and neat tale it would be if the story ended there! Unfortunately, from what we can gather, not long after Paul bade his new brothers and sisters in Christ farewell certain "others" came in like wolves in sheep's clothing to re-teach and re-form this tenderly young Christian assembly. In his letter, Paul accuses the Galatians of being too gullible in being hoodwinked and taken in by these rival Christian teachers. *You foolish Galatians! Who has bewitched you?* (3:1). Paul does not name or identify his rivals explicitly and we don't know their identities or background, but on a few occasions in his letter he makes reference to a specific "they": *they* butter you up but only to cook you (4:17)! *They* are throwing you into confusion and want you to act out of fear, not freedom (5:7–12). *They* want to win you as converts to *their* team but don't really care about your faith (6:12–13). Paul's opening salvo gets right to the heart of the matter: *anyone preaching a*

---

4. See A. J. Goddard and S. A. Cummins, "Ill or Ill-Treated? Conflict and Persecution as the Context of Paul's Original Ministry in Galatia (Galatians 4.12–20)," *JSNT* 52 (1993): 93–126.

different gospel of Christ than the one I am preaching is selling a false gospel, an anti-gospel (1:6–9). Now, in the kind of written Greek Paul was using in the first century, there weren't exclamation points (or any punctuation, for that matter)—but if there were, he would be using them liberally throughout 1:6–9!

When Paul was writing to the Galatian Christians, they were at a pivotal juncture in their faith. Paul was alerting them that taking the path of the rival teachers would lead them quickly off a steep cliff to their demise. Indeed, there are signs that they were *already* wandering down that fatal path (hence Paul's "so quickly deserting the one who called you"; 1:6). In that case, Paul was concerned that they might get to a "point of no return," as he says toward the end of the letter: "if you let yourselves be circumcised, Christ will be of no benefit to you" (5:2). The urgency in Paul's tone is clear, as if the Galatians were at the ritual point of knife to skin.

Now, circumcision is a "presenting" issue in this letter, but Paul actually had bigger concerns than the singular act of circumcision. The Galatians' circumcision would be the symptom of the larger problem of rejecting the pure suffi-ciency of Christ and accepting a false gospel and faith. This false gospel claimed to value Christ, but added circumcision (and performing works of the Law) as a necessity. However, Paul saw this "addition" of circumcision as a subtraction which takes away from the work of Christ.

Now, Paul did not have a blanket anti-circumcision pol-icy. According to Acts 16:3, Paul encouraged his colleague Timothy to get circumcised for the sake of ministry among Jews. But the gentile (i.e., non-Jewish) Galatian Christians were taught by the rival teachers that they *must* be circum-cised as a sign of obedience to the Jewish Law—this would secure their relationship with God. From the rival teachers' perspective, circumcision was a necessity even though the

Messiah had already accomplished his work. We will get into more detail later about the logic and theology behind these perspectives at play in the first-century churches, but it suffices to say for now that Paul saw the Galatians' potential acquiescence on the matter of circumcision *not* as merely a ritual of devotion to God, but rather as a symbol of their cutting themselves off from Christ as their umbilical link to God by faith and gospel (5:2–6). They were deciding where to place the weight of their trust: in the person of Christ alone *or* in the Law and its commandments. On this particular occasion, Paul needed to make it clear that you cannot have it both ways: a slave cannot have two different masters. Circumcision, all by itself, can be a matter of personal preference (5:6; 6:15). But if one were to invest in that act *too much*, so that somehow *this* becomes the gospel, then the ritual knife becomes deadly. Paul's letter as a whole is a warning and invitation. It is a warning *not* to give in to fear, and it is an invitation to put full faith in Jesus Christ for true belonging, righteousness, freedom, and hope.

There are some tedious, but important, technical discussions of place and time to consider in order to fill out the picture of what was going on in this letter. Where exactly were the Galatians? It might seem like a question easily solved with a map, but in this case it is not that simple. Some of the ancient Gauls (the original "Galatians") emigrated to Asia Minor in the 3rd century BCE. When this region was conquered by the Romans, "Galatia" was made into a province that covered a wide geographic area not only including the area of the ethnic Galatians, but also other people inhabiting the southern part of the province (like the Lycaonians and Pisidians). Put simply, when Paul refers to the letter recipients as "Galatians" (3:1) it is unclear whether he was specifically referring to ethnic Galatians (northern Galatia) or residents of the province of Galatia (who might live in the southern region and might not be ethnically Galatian). We know from Acts 13–14 that Paul did visit southern Galatia during one of his ministry trips, so that makes it more than possible that he wrote the letter to Christians there. But there is no way to rule out a visit by Paul to northern Galatia. These questions and issues complicate discerning both the destination location and composition date for this letter. Thankfully, not much hangs on this "who" issue for our purposes in this theme volume.

As for the *when* question, we have more pieces of the puzzle, but still no clear picture emerges. There are no comments in the letter itself that identify when Paul wrote it, but there might be some helpful connections between Paul's autobiographical timeline in Galatians and Luke's story of Paul's travels in Acts. In Galatians, Paul mentions two visits to Jerusalem (1:11–24; 2:1–10). Scholars debate if or how these visits match up with information from Acts. Most scholars put the date of the composition of Galatians somewhere in the mid-50s of the first century. Fortunately, not much in this themes book will be dependent on the dating issue.

PAUL'S RIVALS AND THE MATTER OF THE LAW

Not long ago, I was reading Udo Schnelle's big book *The First One Hundred Years of Christianity*.[5] Obviously, the life and ministry of the apostle Paul is going to be a major part of that study. I was expecting that. But what I *wasn't* expecting was a little section he had called "The Counter Mission against

---

5. Udo Schnelle, *The First One Hundred Years of Christianity: An Introduction to Its History, Literature, and Development*, trans. James W. Thompson (Grand Rapids: Baker Academic, 2020).

Paul." It's hard for many of us today to imagine this, since Paul is remembered as the apostolic juggernaut who faithfully guided the expansion of the gospel mission. But Schnelle is right: some Christian leaders, including people with significant resources and influence, saw Paul's apostolic ministry as a threat, and they actively sought to undermine his work. It is obvious when you read Paul's letter to the Galatians that he was trying to counteract the influence of rivals, whom scholars sometimes refer to as the "Teachers," the "Missionaries," or the "Agitators." Paul talks about *some* who were throwing the Galatians into confusion and perverting the gospel (1:7). These rivals apparently came to Galatia to compel the gentile Christians to demonstrate their commitment to the Jewish Law by getting circumcised (5:3; cf. 2:3). They believed that the Galatian Christians could not truly be children of God without living under the Jewish Law (4:21; 5:4). They may have also impressed upon them the necessity of observing Jewish religious holidays (4:10).

Based on Paul's reaction in the letter, it appears that the church was genuinely tempted to buy into the rivals' version of the gospel, obligating its members to obey the Jewish Law (3:1; 5:2–6). Paul warns his readers that this path would not lead to joy and freedom, but rather fear and bondage: "For freedom Christ has set us free. Stand firm, therefore, and do not submit again to a yoke of slavery" (5:1). To be clear, Paul was not against reading or learning divine wisdom from the Jewish Law and what we call the Old Testament. Far from it—indeed, he cites from the Old Testament approvingly and treats it as the Word of God throughout his letter. So, the matter seems to hinge on whether believers in Jesus are obligated to obey the Jewish Law in order to be right with God. Paul's answer is a clear "no." In the end, though, he does not specifically oppose circumcision. It is not the act of circumcision (alone) that would cut believers off from Christ. (Paul was circumcised, after all!) Rather, it is the power one gives to circumcision to serve as some kind of protective ritual, a marker of salvation, or a badge of righteousness. Paul resists this temptation because *only Christ* can make one righteous (2:16–21; 3:21–22; 6:14).

APPROACHES TO THE LAW IN PAUL'S THOUGHT

As the previous discussion has made clear, the Law—and how Christians relate to the Law—are key issues in this letter and a matter of rigorous debate among Pauline scholars. Paul clearly respects the Word of God given to his people, the Jews, and he cites Scripture as divine instruction in Galatians. He expects believers to listen to and obey God's Word according to the Old Testament (4:21). And yet he also talks about how he died to the Law (2:19), how reliance on the Law brings a curse (3:10, 13), that the Law does not come from "faith" (3:12), and that the Law and the Abrahamic promise are at odds in some way (3:17–18). But Paul firmly denies that the Law opposes the promises of God (3:21). And then, again, he says that Christ came to free people from the Law (4:4–5). And he writes in a tantalizingly brief statement about the "law of Christ" (6:2). It can feel like a dizzying exercise to try to follow Paul's argument about the posture of Christians toward the Jewish Law. It is no surprise, then, that scholars have devised different approaches to discerning the core convictions and ideas that drive Paul's reasoning and discourses in this important letter. At the risk of over-simplification, we will look at four different (but not always mutually exclusive) perspectives on Paul's master messages about the Law.

Law Is about Doing, Faith Is about Believing in Jesus (The Reformation Approach)

This theme or headline is a classic approach to Galatians, and is especially associated with constructs and arguments from the Reformers and like-minded scholars today. According to this approach, Paul critiques obedience to the Law as a way of becoming righteous before God because it focuses on working and doing. Instead, the true path to justification is by *faith* in Jesus Christ—believing and relying on Christ alone. For example, early twentieth-century scholar George Findlay explained justification by faith as the "soul's recumbency on Christ," resting and relying on the finished work of Christ rather than the works of one's own self.[6] This approach draws from passages in Galatians where Paul is specifically juxtaposing "works of the law" and "faith" (2:16–17; 3:12; cf. Rom 3:27; 4:5). The problem with this approach is that it doesn't make much sense of why God would give a (doing) Law in the first place; furthermore, Paul seems to combine believing and doing in Galatians (5:6: "faith *working* through love"; 6:10) and elsewhere (Rom 1:5; 1 Thess 1:3; 2 Thess 1:11), which complicates the argument for one (faith) versus another (doing).[7]

The Law Forms and Protects Israel, but Marginalizes Gentiles (The New Perspective on Paul)

In the last quarter of the twentieth century, the hot debate in Pauline studies was the "New Perspective on Paul." It is not so new anymore, but that conversation has still shaped the

---

6. G. G. Findlay, *The Epistle to the Galatians* (New York: A. C. Armstrong, 1889), 228.

7. This believing vs. doing dichotomy is especially prominent in the work of Douglas Moo; see Douglas J. Moo, *Galatians*, BECNT (Grand Rapids: Baker Academic, 2013); also *A Theology of Paul and His Letters: The Gift of the New Realm in Christ* (Grand Rapids: Zondervan Academic, 2021). For counter-arguments, see Nijay K. Gupta, *Paul and the Language of Faith* (Grand Rapids: Eerdmans, 2020).

modern study of Galatians. It's hard to summarize the "NPP" in a nutshell, but we'll just flag here a key aspect that relates to Paul and the Law in Galatians.[8] Scholars like James D. G. Dunn have argued that after meeting Christ and being called as apostle to the gentiles, Paul came to see that the covenant Law of Israel was oriented toward one ethnic people. Part of what God was doing in Christ in this new era was welcoming gentiles into the family of God *as* gentiles, without them having to *first* become Jews or conform to Jewishness in order to be justified.

This helps to explain several things in Galatians, such as the emphasis on circumcision. *Why circumcision?* Because this was a key ritual that marked Jews *as* Jews (God's special and holy people) within Israel and also in the eyes of outsiders. So, too, the Jewish observance of food laws and religious days and festivals. Notice also how Paul says that "Scripture," foreseeing that God would justify gentiles by faith, preached the good news in advance to Abraham saying, "All the Gentiles shall be blessed in you" (3:8). In this statement the "gospel" that was preached to Abraham was not about faith/works, believing/doing, heaven, or even (explicitly) about the Messiah. But rather it promised that Abraham's family would expand to include all the nations.

Now, there has been strong pushback against the New Perspective on Paul, and it is worth stating that not all of those who are identified with the New Perspective read Galatians in exactly the same way.[9] But the substance of the critique of

---

8. For those looking for a brief summary, see Kent L. Yinger, *The New Perspective on Paul: An Introduction* (Eugene, OR: Cascade, 2011).

9. To get a good sense for different approaches to Paul, including the New Perspective and critics of the New Perspective, I highly recommend Scot McKnight and B. J. Oropeza, *Perspectives on Paul: Five Views* (Grand Rapids: Baker Academic, 2020); for a more concise treatment, Nijay K. Gupta, *A Beginner's Guide to New Testament Studies: Understanding Key Debates* (Grand Rapids: Baker Academic, 2020), 57–86.

this view is that it runs the risk of reducing Paul's gospel to social unity, cultural inclusion, and mutuality. However, does Paul want to say more in this letter than that?

The Law Given by God Was Corrupted by Sin and Death (The Apocalyptic Paul Approach)

On the more negative end of interpretations of Paul's view of the Law, we have some scholars who argue that Paul came to see the Law as co-opted by evil forces and therefore dangerous for believers. For example, in Galatians 3 Paul mentions that the Law was "ordained through angels by a mediator" (v. 19). Why does Paul mention angels here? One theory reads this as implying that, against God's intended purposes, nefarious beings "tampered" with his covenant, imposing the Law on Israel so it would provoke transgressions rather than restrain them.[10] If this view is correct, it could explain why Paul says the Law did not originate from "faith" (3:12) and that Law obedience brings a divine curse. But this approach also leaves too many questions: *Why would God not intervene to stop the angels? Why is the Law proclaimed so universally in the Old Testament as wise and beneficial? Why would Paul tell the Romans that the Law is (still) righteous, good, and holy (Rom 7:12)?*

The Law Protected Israel for a Time before Christ, but Now That Era Is Over (The Salvation-Historical Approach)

Another popular approach to Paul's perspective on the Law in Galatians focuses on eschatology and salvation history. The Law was given by God to support and guide his people, but the problem is that it has its limitations. It was never designed to make sinners righteous; rather, it was meant to

---

10. Martinus de Boer, *Galatians: A Commentary*, New Testament Library (Louisville: Westminster John Knox Press, 2011), 230–31.

confine Israel in a kind of "holding pattern" until the Messiah would come to initiate a new covenant, in which the people's sinful hearts would be changed. This approach seems to track with the analogies that Paul uses in Galatians 3. For instance, Israel had been given the Law as a *paidagogos* until the coming of Christ. The household *paidagogos* was a male slave that functioned like a combination of a nanny, tutor, companion, and disciplinarian. He accompanied minors until they came of age, keeping them safe and helping them grow up, but also punishing them whenever they misbehaved. Once the time came and the children were grown, they would no longer live under the power of the *paidagogos*.

Scholars have debated whether Paul's use of this image reflects negatively or positively on the Law. But it is probably best to set those specific questions aside and observe that Paul's point is that the *paidagogos*, whatever his benefits or drawbacks, was a *temporary* companion and guardian. Paul draws a somewhat similar analogy in chapter four: "heirs, as long as they are minors . . . remain under guardians and trustees until the date set by the father" (4:1–3). Here, Paul is talking about living under the "elemental spirits of the world" (which may or may not be related to the Law, depending on one's interpretation), but he goes on to mention that when the "fullness of time had come" God sent his Son Jesus to redeem those under the Law (4:4–5). Paul thus views the era of the Messiah as a kind of "coming of age" for the people of God, both Jew and gentile.

Summing Up

These views on Paul and the Law continue to be discussed and debated. Again, they are not all mutually exclusive, but leaning into one of these approaches leads to a particular kind of reading of Galatians, and promoting another one presents a different reading, sometimes *starkly* different. To lay my own cards out on the table, I am hesitant to adopt approaches that reflect negatively on the Law and reinforce too sharp of a disjunction between the Law and Christian faith. Paul's concern was not with the Law per se, but with a misuse of the Law and any approach to the Law that would undermine the centrality of Christ in the era of fulfillment. Personally, I find that a combination of the New Perspective and Salvation-Historical readings offer the most compelling approaches to making sense of the theology of Galatians.

The primary focus of this academic series (New Word Biblical Themes) is an explication of the theological themes of the New Testament texts, and we will get to those pertaining to Galatians shortly, but I find it beneficial to first present a brief run-through of the text to show how Paul's argumentation flows. Themes don't exist in a vacuum; they pervade a continuous discourse, whether it be a gospel, epistle, historical novel, or apocalypse. Here I will offer in brief my exposition of Galatians; to read a more expanded discussion, I encourage you to look at my volume on Galatians in the Zondervan Story of God Bible Commentary series.[11]

STRUCTURE AND FLOW OF GALATIANS

Committed to the True Gospel (1:1–1:10)

In some ways, Galatians reflects typical features of Paul's letter openings. He introduces himself (1:1) and addresses the recipients (1:2) with an initial blessing (1:3). He then offers "color-commentary" descriptions that clue the reader in to some of the letter's main concerns and topics. Paul underscores his apostolic position and mission—he was not

---

11. Nijay K. Gupta, *Galatians*, SGBC (Grand Rapids: Zondervan, 2023).

appointed by any human leader or committee, but by Jesus
Christ and God the Father (1:1). There is perhaps here a tin-
gle of defensiveness in Paul's writing voice, fending off any
whispers that he can only be recognized by certain Jerusalem
leaders. He will return to his personal story in 1:11–2:21,
demonstrating how he has followed the voice and leading
of Jesus Christ step-by-step. He was not a Jerusalem-trained
apostle gone rogue; he was a slave of Jesus Christ who served
his Lord faithfully.

In 1:6–10, Paul skips any sort of "thanksgiving" statement
that one typically expects and launches directly into his
shock and disappointment at the Galatian Christians' all-of-
a-sudden equivocation over the gospel he had preached to
them. "Some" people (1:7) had come into their midst and
preached what Paul considered a counterfeit gospel, and part
of their pitch was likely to question Paul himself. Perhaps
they accused Paul of being a people-pleaser—a huckster
who just tells people what they want to hear—attempting to
get the Galatians to buy his gospel, which *they* thought was
incomplete. In response to this, Paul affirms his faithful commitment and his genuine message and ministry—and he has
the scars to prove it: "If I were still pleasing people, I would
not be a slave of Christ" (1:10, my translation).

Paul's Unique and Independent Calling (1:11–24)

Galatians is clearly one of the most autobiographical of
Paul's letters. In other epistles we gather bits and pieces of
Paul's personal story, but here we have an extended "flash-
back" to his life before and then after meeting Christ. Why?
This personal narrative is not a digression. Paul's purpose
seems to be twofold. First, he needed to demonstrate that he
had been guided by Jesus Christ from beginning to end; he
did not make up his apostolic message and mission for his

own benefit. He was called from above to preach the gospel, and he had been faithful to follow God's leading despite not coming to his calling in the more traditional way of the other apostles. Second, Paul's story reveals how he had been committed from the beginning to welcoming gentiles into the family of God through Jesus Christ, *as gentiles*, without the obligation of circumcision or mandatory adherence to the Jewish Law.

Paul talks about his past life *before*—when he focused on passionately persecuting the church (1:13). As a Pharisee, Paul was zealous for purifying the people of God in accordance with his traditions. And he admits he was good at it! But God himself put a stop to Paul's violent activity and revealed to him both the true identity of Jesus (the Son of God) and Paul's unique calling to become an apostle to *embrace* gentiles, rather than to protect Israel *from* them.

In 1:16b–24, Paul makes it clear that his first instinct after becoming a believer was not to run straight to Jerusalem to learn from the apostles. And when he did go there, he went to make contact with Cephas (Peter) and become acquainted with him, not to receive specific apostolic training or even to gain his stamp of approval. Paul did not go to Jerusalem to join Cephas's team, but to get up to speed on what God was doing in the worldwide gospel mission.

The Gentile Mission and Defending the Truth of the Gospel (2:1–10)

Paul narrates a second, more "official" visit to Jerusalem in the opening of the second chapter. But he was not alone. Accompanied by his friend Barnabas and his apprentice Titus, Paul explained to the leadership there the gentile mission to which he was called by Jesus Christ. A central aspect of Paul's message and ministry is clearly that gentiles do not have to be circumcised to be right with God in Jesus Christ (2:3). Titus was put forth as a kind of "case study": he was not a Jew, and Paul saw no reason for him to be circumcised. However, there was disagreement at this summit. Presumably, some attendees argued that gentiles ought to respect Jewish tradition and become circumcised. While there appeared to be a heated debate fueled by interlopers, the apostles ultimately recognized the unique and divine calling on Paul and extended the right hand of fellowship. They decided that Cephas would oversee the mission to Jews (the "circumcised") and Paul to the gentiles (the "uncircumcised"). There was no negotiation or debate about this; Paul did not have to budge on what he was called to. The apostles only encouraged him to "remember the poor," a concern he shared with them (2:10).

Why did Paul go into such detail about this meeting a long time ago in a city far, far away from Galatia? With a bit of imagination, we can make some guesses at the rumors that were spreading about Paul; this was his opportunity to clear the air. Many scholars propose the following scenario: The rivals in Galatia were calling Paul into question, arguing that he couldn't be trusted; that he was a chameleon, saying whatever people wanted to hear to increase his own popularity and power. But, Paul argues in response, nothing could be further from the truth. From the moment he met Christ, he has not strayed from the path he was set on—ministering to gentiles—and this crucial Jerusalem meeting had secured the cooperation of the key Judean leaders, the apostles.

By Faith in Christ, Not Works of the Law (2:11–21)

Paul transitions to another incident, 700 km north of Jerusalem, in the city of Antioch. He and Barnabas were there doing ministry (see Acts 11:19–30), and Cephas showed up (2:11). Apparently, there was a mixture of Jewish and gentile

Christians in Antioch, and at first Cephas intermingled among them, taking dinner invitations from both Jewish groups and gentile ones. But then "certain people came from James" (2:12) and intimidated Cephas, so he distanced himself from gentile believers, no longer eating with them. Cephas's influence was so powerful that even Barnabas joined in this hypocrisy, preaching oneness and equality in faith but refraining from table fellowship with gentiles (2:13). Consequently, these gentile believers felt like second-class citizens among the people of God.

Paul would not accept this, so he called Cephas out publicly, charging him with acting out of step with true Christian belief (2:11). As Paul emphasized, Jews who believe in Jesus Christ know full well that justification—becoming right with God—cannot come through performance of works of the Law, but through faith (2:16). Obviously, Cephas, one of Jesus's own first followers, knew this. So, the issue was more a matter of understanding how behavior and belief match up.

Paul expresses what I consider to be the heart of his theology and gospel in this passage: "I have been crucified with Christ; and it is no longer I who live, but it is Christ who lives in me. And the life I now live in the flesh I live by faith in the Son of God, who loved me and gave himself for me" (2:19–20). Those who belong to Christ are dead to the Law, dead to sin and death, dead to fear, and dead to self. Living in the love of Christ means living a new life of faith, no longer under the Law. That doesn't mean Paul repudiated everything to do with the Law. He encourages the Galatians to "listen" to the Law (4:21). But works of the Law (like circumcision and food and table practices) do not dictate the behavior of believers, who live in real-time responsiveness to Jesus Christ and walk in the footsteps of the Spirit (5:25).

The Blessing of Abraham and the
Promise of the Spirit (3:1–14)

"You foolish Galatians!" Paul begins chapter three with a word of astonishment, disappointment, and urgency (3:1a). Clearly, he transitions from the past (Jerusalem visits, Antioch) to the present, and right into the faces of the Galatians. He hits them with a barrage of questions: *How did you receive the Spirit—works of the Law or faith? Did you start with the Spirit, now to end with flesh? Did God's Spirit do amazing things in your midst because of works of the Law, or faith?* When Paul had left the Galatian believers, we can presume that he thought they were on a great track with their faith. But they now appeared to have deviated significantly and were on their way to ruin. The Galatians had earlier walked by faith in freedom and joy; now they were clinging to works of the Law and living into fear.

To help his readers reset their faith, Paul harks back to the prototypical story of Abraham. Abraham's *faith* in God had enabled him to become right with God (3:6). Thus, those who want to join Abraham's family must live according to that same faith. Relying on observing the Law to be right with God brings a curse—here Paul quotes Deuteronomy 27:26: "Cursed is everyone who does not observe and obey all the things written in the book of the law" (3:10). It does not mean that what the Old Testament Law says is bad. Instead, it means that the Law is a path that once guided Israel in its covenant, but now it is no longer a path meant for believers because Christ has come. Indeed, the Law was never a path meant to lead to justification before God. Paul finds the more permanent or eternal covenantal dynamic in Habakkuk 2:4: "The one who is righteous will live by faith" (3:11). Indeed, we find the seed of the gospel in Abraham's story: that gentiles are welcome in God's family through the promise of the Spirit, which comes only through faith in the person and promise of God (3:14).

Putting the Law in Its Place (3:15–29)

Paul extends his discussion of Law and promise in the remainder of chapter three. First, he explains that the special promise given to Abraham (which blesses gentiles) came prior to the Law and cannot be changed, canceled, or qualified by the Law (3:15–18). God promised Abraham that all families of the world would be blessed through him by *faith*, not by works of the Law.

This inevitably leads to the question: *Why then the Law* (3:19)? Paul's answer is concise and elliptical, and thus open to several interpretations. He writes, "because of transgressions." This could mean (a) to lessen transgressions, (b) to identify transgressions, or (c) to increase transgressions (see Rom 5:20). In order to determine which of these options is best, one has to work out Paul's theology of the Law and the progression of salvation history, a monumental task we cannot hope to accomplish here.[12] My own conclusion is that (a) and (b) are probably what Paul had in mind.

While Paul's statement about the Law in 3:19 remains opaque, his next point is clear. The Law was given *until* the promise could be fulfilled (3:19c). It was given as a mediation for Israel, but ultimately God desired an unmediated and direct relationship with his people, like what he had with Abraham once upon a time. Paul is insistent that the Law was not bad and should not be viewed as the enemy of promise or faith (3:21). It had its unique purpose and place, but where it becomes dangerous and even destructive is when it is made

---

12. For a more detailed discussion of these interpretive options, see Gupta, *Galatians*, SGBC, 132–50.

to do the job of making someone right with God. It cannot (3:21c).

Adoption into God's family only comes through faith in Christ Jesus, for those who are baptized into him and wrap him around themselves like a garment (3:27). Identifications like "Jew" or "gentile" do not make anyone closer to God per se; all have equal access to the Father and all can call Abraham "father" because of God's promise fulfilled by the Spirit in Jesus (3:27–29).

Heirs through the Son (4:1–11)

Having talked about the Abrahamic inheritance through-out chapter three, Paul begins the next chapter by offer-ing another analogy that explains the new era beyond the administrative role of the Law. Imagine if the people of God are like a male child of a household. While he is young, he is looked after by guardians (4:1–2). Though he has the potential to live as a free person, he is not yet old enough to act independently. The same is true with the Law, which was a system designed to hold Israel in trust. However, at the "fullness of time" Christ, the unique and true Son of God, came to make a new way to redeem those who were under the Law (4:4–5). The Spirit bonds these faith-children to the family, so that through the Son they can call out, "Abba! (Father)!"

In 4:7 Paul points out the difference between being a slave, beholden to the Law and without inheritance, and a true son. This leads into a teaching on enslavement as it pertains to the Galatians. Earlier, Paul had mentioned how the Galatians were enslaved to the *stoicheia tou kosmou*, "the elemental spirits of the world." It is hard to understand today exactly what Paul meant by this phrase, but it appears to refer to the raw elements of the world such as earth, wind, water, and fire.[13] Paul was not necessarily talking about these elements as gods, but rather how these primal elements were understood to regulate time and religious activity—for example, ritual time controlled by the movement of the sun and moon. The Galatians, before knowing Christ, had worshiped the classic Greco-Roman gods as well as local deities. Their traditions and rituals would have been dictated by elemental forces that demanded their allegiance. Paul is emphasizing that such practices are carried out from fear and obligation. The Galatians have been freed from this fear—how can they now be intimidated into a new set of fears (4:8–10)?

Am I Your Enemy? (4:12–20)

Paul steps back from the flow of his arguments about Law and promise to make a more personal statement and appeal. He reminds the Galatians how he came to them in weakness, which could have been an obstacle to their reception of him. But they did not despise or reject him; instead, they warmly embraced him (4:13–14). However, Paul confesses, now they have pulled away and listened to rumors that have hurt their relationship: "Have I now become your enemy by telling you the truth?" (4:16).

Paul directly calls out the rival teachers as false confidants. They don't have the Galatians' best interests at heart and can't be trusted. They don't want the Galatians to be secure heirs, but only outsiders longing to be included. Paul expresses a desperate longing: "My little children, for whom I am again in the pain of childbirth until Christ is formed in you" (4:19).

---

13. See Gupta, *Galatians*, SGBC, 161–69.

A Tale of Two Sons (4:21–31)

As Paul steps back into his flurry of scriptural arguments, he ends with an allegorical reading of the story of Sarah and Hagar from the Old Testament. While Paul's interpretive choices here seem mystifying and perplexing, we can start with the clearest point: he wanted to talk about Abraham and his true children. Paul reminds the Galatians that Abraham's family tree splits with his two sons—one son was born from Hagar, the other from Sarah. Paul talks about these two lines as two separate covenants. Since Hagar was a household slave, and Ishmael was born through natural means and human decision, Paul references the "child of the slave . . . born according to the flesh" (4:23a). On the other side of the family tree is Isaac, "the child of the free woman . . . born through the promise" (4:23b). Scholars have sometimes viewed these two covenants as Judaism (slavery, flesh) and Christianity (freedom, promise/Spirit). But Paul wasn't repudiating or denying "Judaism"; he was specifically rejecting the teaching of the false *Christian* teachers who were promoting circumcision and works of the Law.

The climactic appeal of this section comes with Paul's citation of Genesis 21:10: "Drive out the slave and her child" (4:30). In Genesis, these are the words of Sarah who wants Hagar and Ishmael removed. God does affirm Sarah's wish, but he confirms to Abraham that Ishmael, though rejected, will still thrive. Paul draws from these words a warning to the Galatians to distance themselves from any influence that might seek to threaten their status as already-free members of God's household.

Slavery under the Law, Freedom in Christ (5:1–15)

From the more explanatory arguments of chapters three and four, Paul changes gears to the final major section of his letter, chapters five and six, where he makes more direct exhortations to the Galatians—the "so-whats" of the letter. The first verse, 5:1, is a bridge from the Hagar/Sarah "two covenants" discourse to Paul's ultimate hope for the Galatian Christians: "For freedom Christ has set us free. Stand firm, therefore, and do not submit again to a yoke of slavery." For the first time, Paul makes explicit the key issue behind the letter: the Galatian believers' consideration of circumcision. The rival teachers had apparently urged the Galatians to quickly move forward with this ritual of inclusion into the Jewish covenant and inheritance, and the believers were contemplating some kind of group adherence to this act. However, Paul does not interpret this move as a harmless act of solidarity with the Jewish people, but rather views it as a choice to cut themselves off from Christ and the way of faith and hope (5:4–5). Paul makes it clear that this isn't merely about the cutting of flesh—circumcision and uncircumcision are not what is really important to God—but about what God ultimately wants: true faith in Christ that is known and realized in love (5:6).

The second part of this section (5:7–12) is another digression that offers a more personal appeal to the Galatians. It is dripping with *pathos*: "You were running well; who prevented you from obeying the truth?" (5:7). Paul pleads with the Galatians to recognize the pretenses of the rival teachers: they want to win the Galatians away from Paul. They present themselves as the heroes and Paul as the villain. Paul, on the other hand, wants to expose them as false teachers.

Next, Paul returns again to the theme of freedom (5:13–15). He reaffirms that freedom in Christ is a gift, and should not be exploited for selfish gain. Freedom from God is also a calling to commit oneself to others in love. The fleshly way of the rival teachers has not brought them hope and joy, but only fear and division (5:15). In contrast, the true mark of the Spirit's transformative presence and work is love.

Live by the Spirit, Not the Flesh (5:16–26)

In this section of the letter, Paul presents two ways of living: by the Spirit and by the Flesh.[14] Paul portrays these as if they are two powers or masters, and they are enemies. The Flesh is associated with subjection to the Law and a way that is finite, which will ultimately disappear. The Spirit, in contrast, is associated with what is eternal and filled with power and goodness. Paul wants the Galatians to evaluate the lifestyle of the rival teachers and look for marks of fleshly living: strife, jealousy, anger, and acting in ways that are impulsive and out of control—such things do not reflect the kingdom of God (5:19–21).

Alternatively, Paul presents the fruit of the Spirit: the winsome and generous ways of Christ that look like love, joy, peace, goodness, and self-control (5:22–23). What was happening in the Galatian community, as a result of the rival teachers' influence, has only brought them division and spite, resulting in a fractured body living into the Flesh.

Imitating the Goodness of God (6:1–10)

In the last chapter of Galatians, Paul continues with his Spirit v. Flesh teaching, exhorting these believers to seek goodness and charity. The Flesh's way leads to competition and point-scoring against one's enemies. On the other hand, the generous way of the Spirit knits together and lifts up the

---

14. We will often capitalize "Flesh," because when Paul uses the language of *sarks*, he is often thinking about more than just skin. He viewed it as a kind of power that overwhelms mortals and leads them into self-centered, desire-driven behavior. Capitalizing "Flesh" reflects that cosmic nature of the Flesh that is often at war with the Spirit (see 5:16–21).

broken. The "law of Christ" is not fulfilled in seeking to justify oneself, to prove oneself righteous over and against the other. Rather, it is fulfilled in bearing one another's burdens (6:2).

In 6:7–10 Paul offers one more passionate appeal for the Galatians to reconsider their abandonment of his gospel: a person can sow to the Flesh and then reap only decay; or sow to the Spirit and reap true life. Only one option leads to goodness and thriving in the community.

Final Words (6:11–18)

As Paul brings this passion-filled letter to a close, his words maintain the urgency of his concerns for the Galatians' well-being. He writes with large letters (6:11), he warns them again about the nefarious motives of the other teachers (6:12), and he directs their hearts and minds to the cross of Christ and the crucifixion of the flesh. He repeats the maxim, "neither circumcision nor uncircumcision is anything" (6:15; cf. 5:6), but this time he adds, "a new creation is everything!" In the end Paul wishes for mercy and peace on all following this rule, and he points to the marks of Jesus that he carries on his own body, probably referencing his identification with Christ as the only ritual mark he needs, in contrast to the rival teachers' promotion of circumcision.

A PREVIEW OF THE REST OF THE BOOK

Having presented a brief overview of the background and content of Galatians in this chapter, in the next one we will engage with key theological conversations related to the theology of Galatians throughout the years. After that, we will address what I consider to be the key theological themes of Galatians: family and belonging in the people of God through Christ (chapter three), faith and participation in

Christ (chapter four), and freedom and slavery in Christ (chapter five). For readers of this book who have followed some of the academic conversations about Galatians and Pauline theology over the last few centuries, you may be surprised that I did not write a chapter on Paul's doctrine of justification by faith. That omission was intentional, though not because I don't think justification by faith is important in Paul's conception and expression of the gospel. It is *very* important, and is clearly a key term in Galatians (especially chapters two and three). However, I thought it would be artificial to treat justification as a kind of free-floating theme. In my understanding of Galatians, Paul's justification language belongs within specific early Jewish and Christian discussions of covenant belonging and one's standing before God. Therefore, I thought it best to subsume my comments on justification under the broader theme of family and belonging (chapter three). However, inevitably justification will come up elsewhere, especially when we discuss Paul's language of faith and participation in Christ (chapter four). In the end, I decided that justification, though not technically a "theme" of Galatians, deserves extended discussion because of the passionate debates over the years and key questions relating to salvation. So I wrote up my thoughts on the nature of Paul's view of "justification" in an appendix (see pp. 129–40).

HOW TO USE THIS BOOK

The Word Biblical series of commentaries and theme books are designed as reference works. As such, I have written this New Word Biblical Themes volume cognizant of the fact that many readers will not read the book from cover to cover, and perhaps not in sequential order. So, later chapters are not necessarily dependent on earlier ones, though I tried to place the theme chapters in order of importance. As another user-friendly feature of the NWBT series, suggested reading will appear at the end of each chapter.

SUGGESTED READING

Boakye, Andrew K., and Peter S. Oakes. *Rethinking Galatians: Paul's Vision of Oneness in the Living Christ.* London: T&T Clark, 2021.

Gorman, Michael J. *Apostle of the Crucified Lord: A Theological Introduction to Paul and His Letters.* Grand Rapids: Eerdmans, 2016.

Longenecker, Bruce W., and Todd D. Still. *Thinking through Paul: A Survey of His Life, Letters, and Theology.* Grand Rapids: Zondervan, 2014.

McKnight, Scot, Lynn H. Cohick, and Nijay K. Gupta, eds. *Dictionary of Paul and His Letters: A Compendium of Contemporary Biblical Scholarship.* 2nd ed. Downers Grove: IVP Academic, 2023.

Silva, Moisés. *Interpreting Galatians: Explorations in Exegetical Method.* 2nd ed. Grand Rapids: Baker Academic, 2001.

RECOMMENDED COMMENTARIES ON GALATIANS

deSilva, David A. *The Letter to the Galatians.* NICNT. Grand Rapids: Eerdmans, 2018.

Dunn, James D. G. *The Epistle to the Galatians.* BNTC. Peabody, MA: Hendrickson, 1993.

Gupta, Nijay K. *Galatians.* SoGBC. Grand Rapids: Zondervan, 2023.

Hays, Richard B. "Galatians." In *The New Interpreter's Bible*, vol. 11, 183–367. Nashville: Abingdon Press, 2002.

Keener, Craig S. *Galatians: A Commentary.* Grand Rapids: Baker Academic, 2019.

Oakes, Peter S. *Galatians.* Paideia. Grand Rapids: Baker Academic, 2015.

ADVANCED RESOURCES

Eastman, Susan. *Recovering Paul's Mother Tongue: Language and Theology in Galatians.* 2nd ed. Eugene, OR: Cascade Books, 2022.

Longenecker, Bruce W. *The Triumph of Abraham's God: The Transformation of Identity in Galatians.* Nashville: Abingdon Press, 1998.

Riches, John K. *Galatians through the Centuries.* Oxford: Wiley-Blackwell, 2008.

CHAPTER 2

Theological Conversations in Scholarship

Before we turn to the key themes in Galatians, it is helpful to paint a broad picture of the theological dynamics involved in this letter. This will facilitate understanding how the themes relate to Paul's conception of God and God's world, and also how the themes interrelate to each other. As we think about the theology of Galatians in this chapter, we must acknowledge that one letter can only tell you so much about a person. It is not so much about what we learn from Paul's theology if we only had this one letter. That would be an impossible task, or at least one that produces little fruit. It is more an examination of how Galatians makes its own distinct contributions to or impressions on the key theological categories. This somewhat synthetic approach to Galatians will offer an important foundation for the themes chapters that follow.

PAUL'S STORY[1]

It makes sense to begin with Paul's understanding of his own story and journey, as that is how he begins the epistle, and

---

1. For a helpful study of Paul's life, see N. T. Wright, *Paul: A Biography* (New

these autobiographical sections take up almost a third of the whole letter. Insofar as his personal calling and integrity seem to be called into question, Paul takes time and care to "set the record straight," as it were. Some may have made it seem like Paul was invited into a Judean apostolic school, and then later went rogue. But Paul was called directly by God and chosen even before he was born (1:15). God set him on the ministry path he has followed.

But, of course, before Paul was God's apostle, he was an enemy of the church, a zealous persecutor of Christians (1:13–14). Yet God chose to reveal his Son, Jesus Christ, to Paul and to call him to preach the gospel to the gentiles (1:15–16).

In Galatians, we see Paul offer "rearview mirror" reflections on his life's story. Two moments seem to be important, though difficult to reconcile. First, Paul mentions that he was a "people pleaser" (1:10). *When? As a young Christian? Or before he met Christ? Which people was he trying to please, and why?* The reference to being a "slave of Christ" as the juxtaposed identity marker leads me to think that his people-pleasing was part of his pre-Christ past. *Did he change from being a people-pleaser to a Christ-pleaser?* Second, Paul addresses accusations that he *still* preaches circumcision (5:11). What does this mean? The "still" (*eti*) implies that Paul did in fact preach circumcision at some point. Assuming this is a true statement about Paul's past, scholars entertain a few possible scenarios. First, it could mean that Paul promoted circumcision among Jews before he met Christ. Yes, it was an expectation of Torah that Jews

---

York: HarperOne, 2018). Over the years, scholars have debated the importance of narrative elements in Paul, including Paul's autobiographical statements; for a rigorous discussion, see Bruce W. Longenecker, ed., *Narrative Dynamics in Paul: A Critical Assessment* (Louisville: Westminster John Knox Press, 2002).

ought to be circumcised at birth, but the reality is that not every male was circumcised. So, perhaps Paul had zeal for this, to promote commitment to the Law among all Israel. But if this is what 5:11 refers to, I can't imagine Paul's opponents really using his former stance against him, questioning his consistency and integrity as a Christian apostle.

A second possibility is that 5:11 refers to ostensible inconsistencies in what Paul prescribes on different occasions. In 1 Corinthians Paul describes his apostolic policy of *adaptability*, assimilating to Jewish culture to win over men and women to the gospel, whether Jews or gentiles (1 Cor 9:19–23). Paul's opponents could have used this accomodationistic practice to accuse Paul of promoting circumcision to the Galatians, since according to Acts 16:1–5 he had encouraged Timothy to become circumcised in order to strengthen his ministry among Jews in Lystra and Iconium.

We also get a brief glimpse into Paul's "earlier life in Judaism" (Gal 1:13a). The word for Judaism here, *Ioudaismos*, does not exclusively refer to a religion. It is better understood as a culture and way of life associated with Jews (which includes religious practices and traditions, among other things). Paul never ceased to be a Jew when he believed in Christ, but this passage does indicate a major shift in his life direction, and he came to regret his former aims of destroying "the church of God" (1:13b). When Paul was focused on *Ioudaismos*, he was growing in prominence and success, making a name for himself among his peers and proving his commitment to Jewish traditions. But God confronted Paul, like a bolt from the blue, and redirected his life. Paul does not present a specific alternative to *Ioudaismos*, but 1:13–24 clearly shows that he shifted from persecutor of the church to preacher of faith in Jesus Christ (1:23).

THE GOD OF THE GOSPEL: FATHER, SON, AND SPIRIT

It should go without saying that Paul was interested in saying something about "God" in his epistle.[2] We cannot presume any sort of conscious and overt Trinitarian articulation of God. We would have to wait a while for the early church to come to a robust understanding of "one God in three persons." And yet Paul does reference "Father," "Son," and "Spirit" as separable entities on the divine side of the line separating heaven and earth, while still apparently maintaining a Jewish understanding of God (which included monotheism). It will become clear in chapter three that family and kinship imagery are central to Paul's conception of religion and covenantal communion with God. So, God (*theos*) is known as "Father" (*pater*) as a prime descriptor, the authority on high who has ultimate power (1:1; 6:7) and also gives grace and peace to his people (1:3). While Christ was seen as the direct agent of salvation, it is clear that Paul thought of God the Father as the person "behind the curtain" who set the agenda for a master plan of redemption (cf. 1:4): "When the fullness of time had come, *God* sent his Son, born of a woman, born under the law, in order to redeem those who were under the law, so that we might receive adoption as children" (4:4–5). And the goal of this redemption was for Christ to make possible redeemed humanity's access and communion with the Father through Christ's unique Sonship, empowered by the Spirit, whereby believers can call out to God, "*Abba!* Father!" (4:6). It is interesting to see a Father-Son-Spirit cooperative dynamic at work here.

---

2. For a helpful study of this subject, see Francois Tolmie's critical engagement with the work of Nils Dahl, N. T. Wright, Richard Hays, Jerome Neyrey, and Christiane Zimmerman; Tolmie, "God in Galatians: Tendencies in the Study of An Important Theme," *Stellenbosch Theological Journal* 4.2 (2018): 265–81.

While God (the Father) is present in the background of Galatians, the God of the gospel watching over his plan as it unfolds, the most discussed divine agent in Paul's text is clearly Jesus Christ.[3] According to 4:4–6 (as just noted), Jesus is the Son who was sent by the Father, and therefore he is a proxy of the Father's activity,[4] but throughout this letter it is apparent that Paul held Son and Father on an equal level, not one above the other in some kind of tiered system of divinity. For example, when Paul makes reference to his commissioning as an apostle, he claims validation simultaneously from Jesus Christ *and* God the Father (1:1). In other letters, Paul mentions the "gospel of God" (presumably God the Father; Rom 1:1; 15:16; 1 Thess 2:8), but in Galatians he talks about the "gospel of Christ" (1:7). And though in one sense Paul can view himself as a slave of God (Rom 6:20–22), it is more common to see the expression "slave of Christ" issue from his pen (1:10; cf. Rom 1:1; 1 Cor 7:22). In some ways, Paul knew Jesus as his "direct report" when it came to obeying and pleasing God. Christ is the active agent who dealt with sin by coming to earth (4:4), bearing sin's curse (3:13–14), sacrificing himself (1:4; 2:19; 3:1), and making a way for new life (6:15).

A key theological dynamic in Galatians is the emphasis on participating in Christ.[5] The gentiles that Paul was typically preaching the gospel to would have readily understood

---

3. See Douglas J. Moo, "The Christology of the Early Pauline Letters," in *Contours of Christology in the New Testament*, ed. Richard N. Longenecker (Grand Rapids: Eerdmans, 2005), 169–92; Gordon D. Fee, "Christology in Galatians," in *Pauline Christology: An Exegetical-Theological Study* (Grand Rapids: Baker Academic, 2007), 207–36.

4. There are some fascinating resonances between these verses (Father sending Son) and Luke's parable of the wicked tenants (20:9–19). We don't have time to explore this here, but what is notable is how a "son" can serve in a unique way as the "father" by extension.

5. See Michael J. Gorman, *Participating in Christ: Explorations in Paul's Theology and Spirituality* (Grand Rapids: Baker Academic, 2019).

certain religious comments that Paul makes about being sent
by God or being a slave of God (or obeying God), but what
certainly would have been perplexing is his language of being
"*in* Christ (Jesus)." Was this some kind of mystical union?
Political cooperation? Or was it a metaphor?[6] In Galatians
3:26–29, Paul talks about believers as "in Christ Jesus" becoming children of God; baptized (literally "dipped") "into
Christ" and clothed "with Christ" (3:27). This is a corporate
experience, as all are *one* in Christ Jesus (3:28). Paul can talk
about this oneness as *belonging* (*hymeis Christou*), a community
associated with Christ (3:29). In fact, Paul can occasionally
talk about union with Christ as a kind of world unto itself:

> For *in Christ Jesus* neither circumcision nor uncircumcision
> counts for anything; the only thing that counts is faith
> working through love. (5:6)

The idea here is that those who live in Christ, who belong
to Christ, live according to a whole new set of standards and
expectations; they operate with a unique worldview and epis-
temology that dictate their value system and, consequently,
their behavior.[7] For Paul, participating in Christ was also an
individual and very *personal* experience.

> For through the law I died to the law, so that I might live to
> God. I have been crucified with Christ; and it is no longer I
> who live, but it is Christ who lives in me. And the life I now

---

6. Richard Hays offers a helpful set of reflections in "What Is 'Real
Participation in Christ?': A Dialogue with E. P. Sanders on Pauline Soteriology,"
in *Redefining First-Century Jewish and Christian Identities: Essays in Honor of Ed Parish
Sanders* (South Bend, IN: University of Notre Dame Press, 2008), 336–51.

7. See J. Louis Martyn, "Apocalyptic Antinomies," in *Theological Issues in the
Letters of Paul* (Edinburgh: T&T Clark, 1997), 111–24; John M. G. Barclay, *Paul
and the Gift* (Grand Rapids: Eerdmans, 2015), 331–448.

live in the flesh I live by faith in the Son of God, who loved me and gave himself for me. (2:19–20)

The life of faith, as Paul describes here, is a life of personal union and communion with Christ Jesus. It is two persons sharing one life together. Similar expressions of intimate union are found in Galatians, such as in chapter one where Paul mentions the revealing of the Son "in me" (1:16), which points to Christ touching the deepest part of Paul's self.[8] Believers are meant to live *in Christ*, but in some sense Christ also resides *in them*. Paul makes this more explicit when he warns the Galatians about the dangers of buying into false teachings about the gospel. Their attraction to the rival teachers could jeopardize their link to Christ (5:2–4). Paul's ultimate desire for his spiritual children is that Christ is formed in them—that their own lives take the shape of Jesus Christ.[9]

The Holy Spirit is also a prominent figure in Galatians, especially in chapters three and five.[10] From Paul's perspective, the Spirit plays a key role in every step of redemption, from initial catalyst (3:2–3) to signs of new life (3:5), deposit of future hope (3:14), spiritual empowerment for the Christian life (4:6), and guidance in walking faithfully with God and resisting the temptations of the flesh (5:16–18; 5:22–23, 25; 6:1, 8).[11] While the Spirit is personalized in some ways in

8. Some translations say "he . . . was pleased to reveal his Son *to* me" (NRSVue), but I side with the majority of translations, which prefer "to reveal his Son *in* me" (NIV, NET). Paul here uses the preposition *en*, which tends to mean "in," though it can mean "to." Here he appears to be talking about not only being the recipient of divine revelation, but also a conduit of it.

9. Scot McKnight, *Pastor Paul: Nurturing a Culture of Christoformity in the Church* (Grand Rapids: Brazos Press, 2019).

10. Interestingly, Paul never refers to the "Holy Spirit" in Galatians; only "Spirit" or "Spirit of [God's] Son."

11. On the Spirit in Galatians, see Jarvis Williams, *The Spirit, Ethics, and Eternal Life: Paul's Vision for the Christian Life in Galatians* (Downers Grove: IVP Academic, 2023).

Paul's letters, the Spirit is also described as a kind of *super-entity* that influences, shapes, empowers, and leads God's people. The Spirit is at the same time a person, a power, and a frame of existence. There is an interesting hinge point in Galatians 3:2: prior to that, Paul's focus in the letter was on the person of Christ and faith in Christ; and once Paul shifts the discussion to the life of the Galatian community, the spotlight moves to the work of the Spirit. This distinction appears to exist because the Spirit "experiencializes" a relationship with God through Jesus Christ (4:5–6). So life with God is in fact life in Christ, and life in Christ is life in Christ *through the Spirit.*

THE GOSPEL: NATURE, IMPACT, AND EFFECTS

It becomes clear early on in this letter that Paul was concerned to have the Galatians get the gospel right. They had fallen prey to false teaching and were on the brink of trading away the true, freedom-giving gospel for a perversion of the Good News, a counterfeit gospel that leads to bondage and alienation from Christ (1:6–10). Before we get into Paul's more constructive teaching on the true nature of the gospel in Galatians, it's helpful to begin with a more basic question: What *is* the gospel?[12] Of course, based on the Greek terminology (*euangelion*), the gospel is a message of good news, particularly the good news of Jesus Christ (1:7).

When Paul refers to his big summit in Jerusalem, he mentions presenting to them the gospel (*euangelion*) he proclaims

---

12. For robust discussions of how the language of "gospel" (*euangelion*) is used in the New Testament, see Scot McKnight, *The King Jesus Gospel: The Original Good News Revisited*, rev. ed. (Grand Rapids: Zondervan, 2016); Matthew W. Bates, *Gospel Allegiance: What Faith in Jesus Misses for Salvation in Christ* (Grand Rapids: Brazos Press, 2019).

(2:2). This appears to be synonymous with his earlier reference to preaching "the faith" (*pistis*; 1:23). As far as Paul's apostolic calling, his mission was to minister to the "uncircumcised" (2:7), i.e., gentiles. He was a divinely commissioned herald of God's blessing to the nations in Jesus Christ (2:6–9).

There are some clues in Galatians that Paul saw the gospel as more than just a message or a teaching; he saw it as a whole world unto itself. He talks about it as if it is a kind of Christian standard, hence the repeated phrase "truth of the gospel" (2:5, 14): the idea that the gospel of Jesus Christ sets up a certain code of conduct for the people of Jesus; a track or pathway of living that falls within a certain moral boundary of gospel living. In fact, when Paul recounts his confrontation with Cephas and how he called him out on "not acting consistently with the truth of the gospel," the main Greek verb here is *orthopodeo*⁻—"to walk straight," that is, to follow the designated path. This word refers to consistency, a lifestyle that corresponds with one's ideology and values; it is the opposite of hypocrisy.[13] Paul was concerned that Cephas and especially those believers influenced by Paul's own ministries think, live, and act consistently with the wisdom and standards of the gospel and lordship of Christ. Needless to say, this applies to the Galatians. In chapter five, Paul warns them about succumbing to the temptation of ritual circumcision. Again, Paul was not against circumcision per se—he himself was circumcised as a Jew. But what he deemed anti-gospel was a compulsion to be circumcised *in order to* be right before God. This obligatory cutting of the flesh would, in effect, "cut" the Galatians off from Christ, because they would be putting their faith in something *other than* Christ (5:2–4).[14]

---

13. Quite possibly, Paul coined this compound verb (*orthopodeō*).

14. This point is especially emphasized in Gordon D. Fee, *Galatians*, Pentecostal Commentary (Dorset, UK: Deo Publishing, 2007).

In contrast, the life of faith in Christ recognizes that neither circumcision nor uncircumcision puts one at an advantage or disadvantage with God. The negative effect of the outside teachers (who question Paul's version of the gospel) is that they have not only perverted the gospel, but also so disoriented the Galatian believers that their "gospel compass" was not working. These believers were struggling with "obeying the truth" of the one true gospel (5:7).

GALATIANS AND THEOLOGICAL APPROACHES TO PAUL

Galatians has been a foundational text in the historical study of Pauline theology, and for good reason. It is widely considered one of Paul's earliest extant letters and therefore reflective of the earliest era of Christianity we have record of. More importantly, it deals with certain false teachings that required Paul to articulate the heart of the gospel with passion and clarity. The nature of the disputes and debated ideas that Paul addresses demanded that he lay out the essentials of the one true gospel and how believers engage with God and the good news of Jesus Christ by faith. While Paul is crystal clear about the centrality of Jesus Christ and the important role of faith (*pistis*), scholars have long debated the theological structures and perspectives that stand behind Paul's expression of the gospel. They also have differed in how one might order some of the key theological terms in importance.[15] We will

---

15. For a thumbnail sketch of the various approaches to Paul's theological perspective, see Nijay K. Gupta, *A Beginner's Guide to New Testament Studies: Understanding Key Debates* (Grand Rapids: Baker Academic, 2020); also Douglas J. Moo, *A Theology of Paul and His Letters: The Gift of the New Realm in Christ* (Grand Rapids: Zondervan Academic, 2021), especially 349–531; N. T. Wright, *Paul and His Recent Interpreters: Some Contemporary Debates* (Minneapolis: Fortress Press, 2015). For a deeper exploration, see Scot McKnight and B. J. Oropeza, eds.,

briefly talk about three perspectives before analyzing how they relate to one another and serve as pieces of the puzzle of Galatians.[16]

Justification and Becoming Right with God

For many Christians today, Galatians is associated with the concept of "justification (by faith)," the idea that believers receive a status of "innocent" through the self-giving death of Christ, the perfect Son of God, on behalf of sinners. While "justification" language *is* prominent in Galatians through the Greek word group *dik**[17] (2:16–17; 2:21; 3:6, 8, 11; 3:21, 24; 5:4), the letter is not about a "forensic" doctrine. We will be discussing Paul's "justification" language at length later on (see especially the appendix, pp. 129–40), but for now it suffices to say that he was not singularly focused on presenting a Christian dogmatics whereby believers are saved by grace and not by works. Paul would have believed that doctrine, of course, and he may have had occasions to teach that corrective lesson, but we ought not to presume that Galatians is primarily a systematic theology. Paul's use of the *dik** language in Galatians is not about (only) being freed from the guilt and penalty of sin; his primary focus in this letter is on being welcomed into the family of God by faith in Jesus Christ. Being "made right with God," i.e., being "justified," is a divine

---

Perspectives on Paul: Five Views (Grand Rapids: Baker Academic, 2020); the five views are Roman Catholic (Brant Pitre), traditional Protestant (A. Andrew Das), New Perspective on Paul (James D. G. Dunn), Paul within Judaism (Magnus Zetterholm), and "Gift Perspective" (John M. G. Barclay).

16. I do not include the New Perspective on Paul in this section, because I see it less as its own theological approach and more as a corrective to certain traditional readings and more narrowly related to Paul's use of the language of works/works of the Law and his engagement with the Old Testament. We will talk about the "NPP" in the next section of this chapter.

17. The related words Paul uses are *dikaioō* (to put right), *dikaios* (righteous, right), and *dikaiosynē* (righteousness, justice, justification).

act of grace that welcomes, embraces, and transforms people. Thus, through the Spirit they bear the fruit of living rightly before God and with friends, neighbors, and even enemies.

The Apocalyptic Invasion and Rescue of God

In the last several decades, there has been a growing interest in the "apocalyptic" approach to Paul's theology, which emphasizes the human plight as enslavement by sin and in need of divine liberation.[18] Scholars like J. Louis Martyn and Martin de Boer have argued that this is the best way to understand Paul's conception of the gospel in Galatians. A key text here would be 1:3–5:

> Grace to you and peace from God our Father and the Lord Jesus Christ, who gave himself for our sins to set us free from the present evil age, according to the will of our God and Father, to whom be the glory forever and ever. Amen.

Christ's voluntary death, from this perspective, is not just an exchange, life (of the Son of God) for life (of the sinner), but an invasion, a heavenly confrontation of sin and evil to reclaim God's world and his people for himself. The "apocalyptic Paul" perspective tends to emphasize divine agency and minimize human agency. For instance, what saves sinners is not human faith, but rather the warfare God wages against evil to set humans free from the "present evil age."

This approach has helped to uncover apocalyptic thinking and language in Paul's letters (like Galatians), but it

---

18. For an important critical analysis of the Apocalyptic Paul perspective and school, see Jamie Davies, *The Apocalyptic Paul: Retrospect and Prospect* (Eugene, OR: Cascade Books, 2022).

would be a mistake to boil Paul's theological conception of the gospel down to one image or construct like "invasion" or "warfare with anti-God powers." For example, Paul's emphasis on faith (*pistis*) throughout Galatians demonstrates that he held an important place for human participation, human belief, and even human choice (to trust), even though one is not saved or justified by faith *itself*. Indeed, faith is how sinners respond to God's rescue and redemption.[19]

Participating in Christ's Death and New Life

A key paradigm that many scholars use for understanding Paul's gospel theology is that of participation in Christ (sometimes called "union with Christ"). Redemption from sin and freedom are not found in some kind of cosmic legal transaction, but in becoming one with Christ by divine grace and through human faith. Now, there is hardly a Pauline scholar I know of who *doesn't* see participation in Christ as central to Paul's understanding and expression of the gospel. The question, though, is how participation is related to other concepts and ideas (like justification, sanctification, etc.). In my own reading of Paul, I see participation in Christ as not only the center of Paul's thought, but the all-consuming concept and "umbrella" under which we put all other theological concepts. With this in mind, I consider 2:19–21 to be the heart of both Paul's message to the Galatians and his theology in general:

> I have been crucified with Christ; and it is no longer I who live, but it is Christ who lives in me. And the life I now live in the flesh I live by faith in the Son of God, who loved me

---

19. See Nijay K. Gupta, *Paul and the Language of Faith* (Grand Rapids: Eerdmans, 2020).

and gave himself for me. I do not nullify the grace of God;
for if justification comes through the law, then Christ died
for nothing.

Believers are not just "justified" or "rescued" by the death
of Christ, but they actually enter into that crucifixion with
Christ and put their sinful old selves to death. What emerges
is a new life with Christ that is lived by faith. Redemption is not
simply *given* by Christ in the gospel; redemption *is* Christ and is
known, accepted, and experienced by faith in a living relationship with Christ. This relates closely to Paul's direct concern
about circumcision in the Galatian church. If these gentile
believers embrace circumcision as a means of righteousness,
this effectively releases their grip of Christ. Either they cling
to Christ, or they accept circumcision; they cannot have it
both ways. This is not because circumcision all by itself is anti-
gospel. Paul does make it clear (twice) in his letter that neither
circumcision nor uncircumcision carries a special meaning
all by itself before God (5:6; 6:15). What *ultimately* matters is
God's work of New Creation through Christ and the Spirit, the
exercising of true faith, and the expression of love for God and
neighbor. True faith is not about impressing God by having the
right checklist of beliefs when you get to the pearly gates. It is
about knowing Christ as fully as possible and being known by
Christ; this takes priority above all other aims and pursuits.

Paul's theology (including his expression of the gospel
and its effects) is dynamic. It cannot be contained by one
construct or metaphor. It focuses on (what I call) the Christ
relation and can be understood using different lenses and
images like sacrifice, rescue, personal reconciliation, transformation, adoption, and inheritance. We would do well to
not limit the theological buffet of Galatians by only dining at
one of the conceptual tables.

JEWISH LAW, ABRAHAMIC PROMISE, AND THE GOSPEL OF JESUS CHRIST

The popular (though inaccurate) notion that Paul dismissed the Jewish Law (and what we call the Old Testament) or, worse, that he rejected it as anti-gospel has persisted in some Christian communities and traditions.[20] Now, one *could* see how this developed if certain statements Paul makes in Galatians were to be taken out of context and collected on a list (especially without looking at many of the positive statements he makes about the Law in other letters, like Romans). For example, in Galatians Paul writes the following:

> . . . a person is justified not by the works of the law but through faith in Jesus Christ . . . because no one will be justified by works of the law. (2:16)

> For through the law I died to the law, so that I might live to God. (2:19a)

> For all who rely on the works of the law are under a curse. (3:10)

> But the law does not rest on faith. (3:12a)

> Christ redeemed us from the curse of the law by becoming a curse for us. (3:13a)

If one were to dwell on these verses in isolation and out of context, Paul could appear to be an enemy of the Jewish Law.

---

20. Patrick Gray offers deep insight from reception history on Paul in his *Paul as a Problem in History and Culture: The Apostle and His Critics through the Centuries* (Grand Rapids: Baker Academic, 2016).

But keep in mind that Paul writes other things which are more positive about the Law and the Old Testament. For example, he quotes extensively from the Old Testament (including the Pentateuch, where we find most of the "laws" of Israel) throughout Galatians, always assuming its ongoing inspiration and authority—all of it is the Word of God for Paul.

In Galatians chapter three, Paul mentions that the Law had a specific purpose in God's plan—"It was added because of transgressions" (3:19). Some scholars take this to mean that the Law was given by God to *increase* sin. I find this inconceivable—why would God trick his people into sinning more and more for many hundreds of years through a gift that was meant to bless them and lead them to righteousness and life (Psalm 19)? I find it more sensible that the Law was given as a blessing to the people of Israel for their benefit, to rein in transgressions. (After all, the Law includes the Ten Commandments and the covenantal command to love one's neighbor.) Paul does not offer his negative comments about the Law in Galatians because he saw the Law as evil or a hindrance to faith per se, but rather he wanted to emphasize that its role—and especially its *limitations*—needed to be fully understood. Apparently the mostly gentile Galatian believers had been influenced by a certain teaching that pressured them to view the Jewish Law as *the means* of becoming right with God and inheriting eternal life. Paul's seemingly harsh statements about the Law in Galatians are not a warning for the Galatian Christians to repudiate the Law; they are Paul's *correction* to false teachings about the Law and the gospel. Paul addresses head-on the interplay between Law and gospel in chapter three:

> Is the law then opposed to the promises of God? Certainly not! For if a law had been given that could make alive, then righteousness would indeed come through the law. (3:21)

The issue for Paul is *not* whether Christians should value the Law, or whether it is relevant or useful. He would not have positively quoted the Law so much unless it was beneficial. Rather, the problem is attributing more to the Law than is necessary—to give the Law a role and expect outcomes that it was never meant to have. The Law was a gift of God for the people of God to serve the promises of God, but the Law *itself* was not meant to be the means of new life.

Paul goes on in Galatians 3 to give an analogy for the good but limited role of the Law in God's plan. As mentioned in chapter one of this book, the Law played a role in an earlier stage of history of something like a *paidagogos* (3:25) for a child in the ancient world. There is no perfect one-word English translation for this Greek term, which referred to a male slave, because we don't really have this kind of person in modern life today. The *paidagogos* was assigned to teach, protect, guide, and discipline the child in his master's household. The Law, by analogy, was given to the people of Israel as a form of the wisdom of God to teach and correct them. But— and here's the main point of Paul's analogy—a *paidagogos* only had a temporary role. The expectation was that the child would "come of age" and enter the maturity of adulthood, learning in the freedom of individual self-determination. To have a *paidagogos* follow you around as a child reflects a clear benefit, protection, and instruction. But to have one follow you around as an adult is an absurdity, as if reverting back to a time of adolescence and immaturity.

Now, this doesn't mean that Paul's analogy requires Christians to cut themselves completely off from the Old Testament. Presumably, a child-turned-adult would no longer need a *paidagogos* in a formal sense, but might still have him as a friend, mentor, and confidant (and not formally a disciplinarian). So, too, in light of the new covenant Paul presented the

Law as Scripture for Christians in a different way; not strictly as "law," but as the wisdom of God for the people of God.[21]

Where does the New Perspective on Paul fit into all of this? In the second half of the twentieth century, a number of scholars were pushing back against antisemitic and anti-Judaic readings of the Bible, especially in regard to Paul. E. P. Sanders wanted to better understand the religious patterns of early Judaism apart from Christian texts and without the bias of classic Christian interpretation that presented the Judaism of Paul's time as primitive, legalistic, and external.[22] Sanders discovered and argued in favor of a genuine understanding of divine grace, mercy, and a covenantal relationship in many Jewish texts (e.g., the Dead Sea scrolls and the Old Testament Pseudepigrapha). Krister Stendahl also made the case that modern Protestants too quickly retroject Martin Luther's "guilty conscience" back into Paul, as if Paul himself struggled with (the "bad religion") Judaism and found grace in (the "good religion") Christianity.[23] James D. G. Dunn took these insights from Sanders and Stendahl seriously and applied them to Galatians.[24] Dunn argued, in particular, that Paul was not making general claims about Judaism as a religion of works (of the Law) versus his Christian religion as a matter of faith. "Works of the Law," Dunn claimed, was a kind of technical phrase, referencing the covenantal command-

21. This is a key argument made by Brian Rosner in *Paul and the Law: Keeping the Commandments of God* (Downers Grove: IVP Academic, 2013).

22. See the classic E. P. Sanders, *Paul and Palestinian Judaism: A Comparison of Patterns of Religion*, 40th anniv. ed. (Minneapolis: Fortress Press, 2017; originally published 1977) and, more recently, Sanders's *Paul: The Apostle's Life, Letters, and Thought* (Minneapolis: Fortress Press, 2015).

23. Krister Stendahl, "The Apostle Paul and the Introspective Conscience of the West," *HTR* 56 (1963): 199–215.

24. See Dunn's collected essays, *The New Perspective on Paul* (Grand Rapids: Eerdmans, 2008) and his *The Theology of Paul's Letter to the Galatians*, NTT (Cambridge; Cambridge University Press, 1993).

ments in the Jewish Law. Jews were obligated to keep these commandments, not to *earn* their salvation but to demonstrate their participation in a covenantal relationship with a gracious God. And certain "works" in particular—such as circumcision and observance of the food laws—became identity badges marking Jews out as Israel, the special people of God. When this understanding was applied to Paul's argument in Galatians, Dunn saw that Paul was not opposing *Judaism* but rather was parrying the false instruction from outside teachers who were trying to compel gentile Galatian Christians to *become Jewish* by taking on the yoke of Torah assigned to Israel. What gives this approach to Galatians strong plausibility is the fact that circumcision and food matters are issues directly addressed in the letter. These were not particularly "good works," and neither Jews nor gentiles thought that one could inherit eternal life through them *as* meritorious deeds.

There has been some pushback against the New Perspective over the years, especially through the concern that some expressions of the New Perspective can be reductionistic, boiling Paul's ministry down to social community development.[25] But, as Dunn has argued numerous times, you can buy into the New Perspective and still emphasize classic Protestant doctrines like justification by faith alone. Ultimately, what many New Perspective advocates are trying to do is read Galatians better in its original context, paying closer attention to the "on the ground" situation. Also, they want to read Paul with a positive sense of his Jewish heritage, viewing his gospel as the fulfillment of the work of the one God rather than as the antithesis to Law or Judaism.

---

25. See D. A. Carson, Peter T. O'Brien, and Mark A. Seifrid, eds., *Justification and Variegated Nomism*, vol. 1: *The Complexities of Second Temple Judaism* (Grand Rapids: Baker Academic, 2001); and idem, *Justification and Variegated Nomism*, vol. 2: *The Paradoxes of Paul* (Grand Rapids: Baker Academic, 2004).

N. T. Wright, also associated with the New Perspective, has affirmed many of the core insights of Sanders, Stendahl, and Dunn, but distinctively brings interest in Abraham to the forefront of the conversation.[26] An older approach might simply focus on Abraham as a model of faith (without works), and Wright would not deny that Paul brings in an element of Abraham as a man who trusted God. But a key piece of the puzzle is sometimes left out: the Abrahamic promise of the blessing of many nations. The gospel is not just that sinners can be saved by personal faith, but also that the *gentiles* would be welcomed into the family of God by faith in Jesus Christ, apart from works of the Law (3:6–9). Gentile believers have an equal share in the inheritance because of Jesus Christ.

A newer view has emerged called "Paul within Judaism."[27] Generally speaking, this group of scholars views Paul as committed to his Jewish faith and people even as a believer in Jesus. When he met Christ and committed himself to Christ, he did not forsake his observance of the Law. As a "Christian," Paul was not *outside* his inherited Judaism, but *within* it. If this is the case, then Paul never spoke against the Law. Rather, he would have promoted the Law as a covenantal obligation for Jewish believers (like himself), but taught that gentile believers were not required to observe the Law. In the case of Galatians, the Paul-within-Judaism scholars argue that when Paul makes negative statements about the Law, we need to take into consideration the context and audience, i.e., pressures on gentile believers to obey the Law. These scholars feel that Paul would have written quite differently to Jewish believers. I do agree that audience matters, and we ought to

---

26. N. T. Wright, *Paul and the Faithfulness of God* (Minneapolis: Fortress Press, 2013).

27. See Mark D. Nanos and Magnus Zetterholm, eds., *Paul within Judaism: Restoring the First-Century Context to the Apostle* (Minneapolis: Fortress Press, 2015).

piece together the audience as best we can, but I think what Paul writes about the Law has a general quality, as with his *paidagogos* analogy. It is clear to me that Paul didn't think the Law had to give way to Christ only for gentiles; after all, they didn't have the Law to begin with! Rather, he was painting with broad brushstrokes about how the (Jewish and gentile) people of God have a whole new relationship to the Law now that the time of fulfillment has come.[28]

I think a beneficial contribution from the Paul-within-Judaism view is the notion that Paul did not see some kind of clear break between "Judaism" and "Christianity."[29] His faith was a very *Jewish* faith in the sense that he worshipped the same God (albeit with a new Christ-centered orientation), utilized the same Scriptures for teaching and guidance, and structured his world in terms of covenant and eschatology.

LIFE IN THE GOSPEL COMMUNITY

Galatians is not as explicit in its teachings on the nature of the church as some of Paul's other letters. For example, Paul does not use the "body" analogy, and he does not touch on offices, roles, and responsibilities in the church in a direct way.[30] However, it would be a huge mistake to assume

---

28. For two recent refutations of the "Paul within Judaism" perspective, see Douglas J. Moo, *A Theology of Paul and His Letters: The Gift of the New Realm in Christ* (Grand Rapids: Zondervan Academic, 2021) and Stephen Westerholm, *Romans: Text, Readers, and the History of Interpretation* (Grand Rapids: Eerdmans, 2022).

29. See Gabriele Boccaccini and Carlos A. Segovia, eds., *Paul the Jew: Rereading the Apostle as a Figure of Second Temple Judaism* (Minneapolis: Fortress Press, 2016).

30. However, Paul does include the seemingly random instruction: "Those who are taught the word must share in all good things with their teacher" (6:6). This seems too specific to be a general teaching, and it doesn't appear in any of Paul's other letters; at the same time, it is difficult to discern how it relates to the Galatian crisis or personal responsibility and mutual care in the community (6:1–5).

that Galatians does not offer important instruction on the
church, the gospel community. Rather than giving formal
instruction on ecclesial traditions, Paul offers a vision for a
"flat" (status-neutral) community of mutuality and grace,
which serves and exhorts one another in love and with a
cruciform spirit.

The Family of Faith

We will devote a whole theme chapter to this concept, but
it is worth briefly pointing out here that in Galatians Paul
emphasizes the notion of the gospel community as a family
of God through Jesus the Son of God. Family in Paul's time
involved close blood relationships where relatives looked
after one another and pursued the honor of the whole family. Paul casts a vision for the church as a kinship collective,
a social body where the members are for each other and
work together for the good of the whole. What unites this
corpus mixtum is not blood, physical resemblance, or ethnic or
geographic origins. All members are one in faith, a people
who believe the same and belong to the same Jesus Christ,
adopted into the household of the great Father through the
only true Son. Paul's family imagery is not just rhetorical
icing on his theological cake; it is structural to the way he
thinks about God and God's people. Conceiving of the gospel
community *as a family* means that the members are *for* one
another, sharing glory and hardship. They are not competing
for honor and leaving each individual to solitarily work out
personal issues.

Eye to Eye, Not Above or Below

"There is no longer Jew or Greek, there is no longer
slave or free, there is no longer male and female" (3:28a).
This verse is often stripped away from its context in Paul's

six-chapter letter and placarded as a political statement. Now, this statement *does* indicate something radical about how Paul considers the person in the New Creation era. However, Paul's point is not about individual status; rather, it is about the ideas that surround this statement: *all who are baptized into Christ and clothed with Christ are one in him, belonging to this faith family as Abraham's children and equal co-heirs of the great covenantal promise of redemption and glory.* At the same time, there is some merit to the argument that Paul may have frequently used this statement in his teaching—note that he talks about not only ethnicity (Jew/Greek) but also legal status (slave/free) and sex (male/female), although the latter issues are not an immediate concern in the Galatian crisis. Paul was not eradicating these forms of personal or group identification—he was cognizant of his own ethnicity, for example. Rather, he was destabilizing the forms of status stratification used in society. In the wider culture, free people were far more important than slaves. Men were more privileged than women. And ethnic rivalries were widespread, as we learn from the interaction between Peter and Cornelius in Acts 10. Paul is clear that this above/below sociology cannot happen in the church. The Christ people, the gospel community, must live eye to eye and shoulder to shoulder, not looking up to or down upon each other, and certainly not stomping on anyone.

Responsible and Generous

We learn in Galatians that another mark of the church is the emphasis on both personal responsibility and other-centered generosity. In 6:2–5, Paul warns the Galatian believers that all people must carry their own load. Every able-bodied individual is expected to take care of themselves and not be an unnecessary burden on anyone else (6:5; cf. 1 Thess 4:11; 2 Thess 3:6–15). This is analogous to the story of the divine manna provision in the wilderness and the instructions to Israel in Exodus 16:13–21. In this test of Israel's faith, every person must only collect what he or she needs, not more (or else others will be deprived of their necessary portion). Paul carried the same mentality toward the church community (2 Cor 8:13–15); this is all about being a respectful and thoughtful member of a commonwealth. Step one is individual responsibility and self-sufficiency. All things being equal, all people should care for themselves. But in reality life is messy and a person's expected reasonable load can become an unreasonable burden. Thus, believers in the household of faith are called to "bear one another's burdens" (6:2), supporting and caring for each other. This requires humility and a generous spirit. The church is expected to be a place of both responsibility (every person carries their own load) and generosity (every person shows attentive love and care to help others who are carrying burdens).

LOOKING AHEAD

In the remainder of this book, we will dive into a few key themes of Galatians, which will flesh out some of the topics we have already touched upon. In particular, we will consider three key themes: family, faith, and freedom. Other important theological topics (like justification, the law, and the Spirit/flesh) will be discussed under these chief themes.

SUGGESTED READING

Dunn, James D. G. *The Theology of Paul the Apostle.* Grand Rapids: Eerdmans, 1998.

———. *The Theology of Paul's Letter to the Galatians.* NTT. Cambridge: Cambridge University Press, 1993.

Elliott, Mark W., Scott J. Hafemann, N. T. Wright, and John
    Frederick, eds. *Galatians and Christian Theology: Justification,
    the Gospel, and Ethics in Paul's Letter.* Grand Rapids: Baker
    Academic, 2014.

Gorman, Michael J. *Apostle of the Crucified Lord: A Theological
    Introduction to Paul and His Letters.* 2nd ed. Grand Rapids:
    Eerdmans, 2017.

McKnight, Scot and B. J. Oropeza, eds. *Perspectives on Paul: Five
    Views.* Grand Rapids: Baker Academic, 2020.

McKnight, Scot, Lynn H. Cohick, and Nijay K. Gupta, eds.
    *Dictionary of Paul and His Letters: A Compendium of Contemporary
    Biblical Scholarship.* 2nd ed. Downers Grove: IVP Academic,
    2023.

Moo, Douglas J. *A Theology of Paul and His Letters: The Gift of the New
    Realm in Christ.* Grand Rapids: Zondervan Academic, 2021.

Novenson, Matthew V., and R. Barry Matlock, eds. *The Oxford
    Handbook of Pauline Studies.* Oxford: Oxford University Press,
    2022.

CHAPTER 3

Family: At Home in the Household of Faith

When most Christians who have been taught historic Protestant doctrine think about the master themes of Galatians, I am sure a few things come immediately to mind. For example, I imagine many would associate Galatians with "justification by faith" and Martin Luther's advocacy for the imputation of Christ's righteousness for sinners. Or maybe Galatians calls to mind "freedom in Christ" over and against slavery to flesh and Law. Eventually, we will be discussing both justification (later in this chapter) and freedom (in chapter five), though with some necessary nuances. But from my own study of the thought and theology behind Paul's letter to the Galatians, I find that the most prominent theme is often ignored (perhaps because it is "hiding in plain sight"?): *family*. I have rarely read introductions and summaries of Galatians that take seriously the kinship and family language appearing frequently throughout all six chapters—so frequently that it seems to dominate Paul's ideas and argumentations in this text. But this theme is too prominent and repeated to be ignored or downplayed. In fact, it is *the* leitmotif of the letter. Put simply, Galatians is about a household community, and especially about *who* counts as part of the family of God and *how*. Paul's bigger picture arguments are twofold:

(1) God's true family does not follow a physical blood line, but a connection through the unique Son Jesus Christ by faith; and (2) God's true family does not recognize tiers of association, with some having more privilege than others (whether Jew or gentile, free or slave, male or female); all who are united with Christ share his unique Sonship privileges. So, Galatians is about *belonging*: belonging to God the Father in the Son Jesus Christ reflects being justified, made right with God; belonging to God implies and protects freedom from slavery; belonging to God energizes faith toward love; and belonging to God requires co-crucifixion with Christ so that Christ can fully live within.

FAMILY LANGUAGE IN GALATIANS

To demonstrate the importance of family language in Galatians, it's helpful to begin at the *end* of the epistle. In 6:7–10, Paul underscores the importance of living by the Spirit and not the Flesh. Perseverance and single-mindedness are required to walk the path of righteousness and integrity, aiming to do what is good and right for all whom you encounter, "and especially for those of the family of faith" (6:10). Paul is conceiving of the whole believing community, Jews and gentiles knit together through Jesus Christ, as one household of God (cf. Eph 2:19; 1 Tim 5:8), "relatives" by faith. Paul's aim was to help the Galatian Christians reconceive the relationships between Jews and gentiles in the church, not in terms of traditional ethnicity (a geographic and blood-based family identity) but as a new kind of family through Jesus Christ. This doesn't do away with ethnic identity, but it does shift priorities—*theological* identity (the family of faith) becomes central to understanding of God, self, and self-in-community.

As we look at Galatians as a whole, we can clearly see the many different expressions and images that Paul uses to imagine these believers as part of one family through Jesus Christ.

"All the brothers"	1:2
brothers and sisters	1:11; 3:15; 5:13; 6:18
The Son (Jesus)	1:16; 4:4
Son of God (Jesus)	2:20
Promised inheritance	3:18
Heirs	3:29
Sonship (Adoption)	4:5
God as *Abba* (Father)	4:6
Heirs and true children	4:7
Children of Abraham	4:21–31
Inheriting the kingdom of God	5:21
The household of faith	6:10

It is easy to glide past this kinship language in Paul's letters, treating it as Christian language of familiarity and affection. But in the ancient world there was nothing more important than the family: the biological and legal family was the essential community for each person. Parents were expected to protect, educate, and guide children; children were meant to obey and honor their parents and support the family business and livelihood. Every person was born with the expectation that they would live to bring honor to their own family and avoid bringing shame upon their relatives and family name. Thus, the Jewish sage Ben Sira counseled, "Do not glorify yourself by dishonoring your father, for your father's dishonor is no glory to you" (Sir 3:10).[1] There was a clear dividing line in society between insiders (members of one's own family group) and outsiders (strangers, foreigners). However, Paul was repeatedly blurring the lines between one biological and ethnic family and another by talking about a new kind of family with a special and precious inheritance. This is the family of God that welcomes any and all who enter through faith in Jesus Christ, the special Son.

It is probably not possible to develop a whole systematic conception of "spiritual" kinship when considering Paul's understanding of the people of God in the Messiah, but enough pieces are in place in Galatians to paint a general picture of what it means to be in the "household of faith."[2] We can sketch it out in this way: *Each of us in the flesh are a part of our biological families with different contexts and dynamics, and have varying levels of power and status through and within our family systems. Some may be promised a great inheritance but others very little, and too many (like slaves) have no future. In contrast, God the Father has offered in his grace a special way into the great heavenly family through the unique Son Jesus Christ. All who enter this family by faith in the Son of God are granted the same rights, privileges, and status as the Son himself. There are no "greater" or "lesser" brothers and sisters, no stepsons or half sisters—all are treated the same as they participate in the life of the Son. An eternal inheritance is guaranteed for everyone: a beautiful name and legacy that will last forever.*

---

1. See David A. deSilva, *Honor, Patronage, Kinship, and Purity: Unlocking New Testament Culture*, 2nd ed. (Downers Grove: IVP Academic, 2022), chapters 5–6.

2. For a study of the importance of metaphors in Paul's thought, see Raymond F. Collins, *The Power of Images in Paul* (Collegeville, MN: Liturgical Press, 2008); for kinship language in particular, see Reidar Aasgaard, *"My Beloved Brothers and Sisters!" Christian Siblingship in Paul* (London: T&T Clark, 2004) and Trevor J. Burke, *Adopted into God's Family: Exploring a Pauline Metaphor* (Downers Grove: IVP Academic, 2006).

When we look at Galatians from this perspective, practically all the other themes in this letter can find their place and sense within Paul's family theology. "Justification," for example, is not first and foremost about "salvation" and some ethereal *eschaton*; it is about divine recognition and affirmation of true belonging, sinners being "right with" God the Father through Jesus Christ. "Freedom," another key theme, is not primarily about getting "off the hook" of the consequences of sin; it is about flourishing in this new household economy, liberated from bondage and integrated into a safe place of flourishing and abundance. "Faith" is not an abstract set of beliefs to assent to; it is the tie that binds this family together, union through knowledge, trust, loyalty, and hope. In the following discussion, we will break down Paul's articulation of the family theme through four images: Father and Son, Justification and Covenant, Adoption and Inheritance, and Brothers and Sisters.

FATHER AND SON

It's easy to overlook the prescripts of Paul's letters—on first glance they can appear to be little more than opening formalities. But (1) Paul tends to adapt these toward previewing or foreshadowing themes in the main body of the letters, and (2) even the smallest or seemingly inconsequential remarks can tell us something about Paul's understanding of God and God's world. We have both of these dynamics in the first few verses of Galatians. Imagine if you were a visitor to a Christian assembly. If Paul's letter to the Galatians was read aloud in this meeting, with those first introductory statements you would begin to formulate your understanding of what being a Christian is all about and how these people think and speak and understand themselves.

Paul an apostle—sent neither by human commission nor from human authorities, but through Jesus Christ and God the Father, who raised him from the dead—and all the members of God's family who are with me,

To the churches of Galatia:

Grace to you and peace from God our Father and the Lord Jesus Christ, who gave himself for our sins to set us free from the present evil age, according to the will of our God and Father, to whom be the glory forever and ever. Amen. (1:1–5)

Paul writes as an *apostolos*—some kind of respected messenger of God, perhaps a prophet, you might surmise. The ancient world saw many false prophets and street magicians who claimed to know the will of the divine, but in reality had learned some clever tricks at a con artist seminar. But this Paul person claimed he was sent by two special divine beings. One is "Jesus Christ," a Jew who was perhaps a great hero turned divine (so a gentile might naturally assume). The other is someone these Christians call "Father," the great celestial patron. At first, it would be unclear how this "Father" and this "Jesus" were connected. But as the letter is read, it becomes clear that these two exist within a Father-Son relationship, which implies unity, intimacy, and oneness of mission and purpose. Paul refers to Jesus four times as "Son" in Galatians ("Son," 1:16; 4:4, 6; "Son of God," 2:20). This is his second most frequent use of this Christological title, after Romans. We do not have the space to explore all the theological dynamics of what it meant to confess Jesus as God's Son, but we can briefly mention a few factors.[3]

---

3. See Amy B. Peeler, "Son of God," in *Dictionary of Paul and His Letters: A Compendium of Contemporary Biblical Scholarship*, ed. Scot McKnight, Lynn H. Cohick, and Nijay K. Gupta, 2nd ed. (Downers Grove: IVP Academic, 2023).

Sonship and the Davidic King of Israel. One of the most prominent thematic resonances of unique sonship language in Jewish thought relates to David, or to a king like David. This is part of the covenantal promise that this ruler will be like a son to God and they will rule over the people together (2 Sam 7:14). Paul almost certainly has this in mind in Romans when he refers to the "gospel concerning [God's] Son, who was descended from David" (Rom 1:3).

Sonship and Israel. The people of God are also recognized as an adopted "son" (hence, "out of Egypt I called my son," Hosea 11:1), and the Israelite king and eventually the Messiah would become the sonship representative of Israel (just as Hosea 11:1 is quoted in Matthew 2:15 in reference to Jesus).

Sonship and Greco-Roman Rulers. In the Greco-Roman world of Paul's time, it was common to refer to the emperor as *divi filius*, "son of (a) god." This indicated status and authority toward the highest level of the Roman stratified universe. New Testament writers, like Paul, who referred to Jesus as Lord (*kyrios*) and Son of God (*huios theou*) were not launching a direct attack against imperial power. Rather, they were positioning this unique Father (God) and Son (Jesus) as the true supreme rulers of the whole world.[4]

Father God and Son Jesus in Communion. What can easily be missed in these complex discussions about Son Christology in the New Testament is the obvious theme of intimacy and close communion between Jesus and his Father that we see when reading the Gospels. We cannot answer with certainty whether Paul was acquainted with "The Four Gospels," but it makes good sense that he knew enough about Jesus's earthly life and teachings to pick up on this familial connection.

---

4. For a thorough study of "divine sonship" in the Greco-Roman world, see Michael Peppard, *The Son of God in the Roman World: Divine Sonship in Its Social and Political Context* (Oxford: Oxford University Press, 2012).

For example, Paul's own use of the early Christian tradition of using Aramaic *Abba* appears to trace back to Jesus himself.

> He said, "*Abba*, Father, for you all things are possible; remove this cup from me; yet, not what I want, but what you want." (Mark 14:36)[5]

> And because you are children, God has sent the Spirit of his Son into our hearts, crying, "*Abba*! Father!" (Gal 4:6)

> For you did not receive a spirit of slavery to fall back into fear, but you have received a spirit of adoption. When we cry, "*Abba*! Father!" (Rom 8:15)

The relationship between these three texts is remarkable. Not only do you have the Aramaic word *Abba* (transliterated into Greek for these original texts) and the addition of the Greek translation "Father" (*patēr*), but these words are also expressed verbally and in very emotion-heavy contexts. It makes sense to me that an *Abba* invocation can be traced back to Jesus himself, indicating that this prayer left an imprint on early Christian liturgy, and Paul also did his part to pass it on.[6]

When we look at Paul's family imagery and themes from this perspective, one of the key ideas conveyed by Father-Son theological language is close agency and intimate association between these two persons. When Paul mentions in

---

5. For a lengthier study of the *Abba* tradition in the New Testament, see Nijay K. Gupta, "The Babylonian Talmud and Mark 14:26–52: *Abba*, Father!," in *Reading Mark in Context: Jesus and Second Temple Judaism*, ed. Ben C. Blackwell, John K. Goodrich, and Jason Maston (Grand Rapids: Zondervan, 2018), 224–30.

6. However, it is worth observing that no other writer (besides Paul and Mark) makes reference to *Abba*.

Galatians, for example, that at the fullness of time "God
sent his Son" (4:4), it seems to be important that this agent
is not just any celestial emissary, but God's own Son.[7] I can't
help but think of the parable of the wicked tenants (Matt
21:33–45), where a group of tenant farmers refused to give
over the harvest profits to the landowner. The landowner
sent slaves to collect these profits, but the farmers killed
them. After another failed attempt, the landowner sent his
own son, his flesh and blood, saying to himself, "They will
respect my son." Instead of honoring the family heir, the
tenants murdered him—but then met the vengeance of the
father. Jesus makes it clear that this story shows communion
between Father and Son, as well as the risk of rejecting the
Son (and facing retribution by the Father). As we return to
Galatians 4:4 after pondering this parable, we see that the
Father's sending the Son shows personal involvement and
investment (the Son is like the Father) and risk (the Son
is precious to the Father). The upshot is this: in Galatians,
Paul's description of Jesus as "Son" is more than mere habit
or convention. Jesus is the beloved Son of the Father, and
he becomes the doorway for believers to enter into the
Father's family.

COVENANT, JUSTIFICATION, AND THE ABRAHAMIC PROMISE

While Galatians has been deemed the epistle of justification (Luther's favorite text and doctrine), this is only worth
observing if "justification" (*dikaiosyne*) is set into the context
of the Jewish covenant and right relation with the God of

---

7. The sending of the Son by the Father is made explicit in several Johannine
texts (John 3:16–17; 5:23; 10:36; 1 John 4:9, 14).

Israel. The doctrine of justification is not about achieving a certain threshold of righteousness or avoiding dropping below a certain marker of sinfulness; ultimately, it is about being in good standing in the covenant (LXX Ps 142:2). Righteous behavior plays a role in this, but the essence of covenantal justification is about being *in the right* with the righteous God. Think about Luke 18, the parable of the Pharisee and the tax collector. The punchline of the story is that the humbled sinner who acknowledges his wrongs goes home "justified," but the self-righteous Pharisee does not (Luke 18:14). Right-doing is not completely irrelevant, but the focus is on covenant faithfulness and a humble and penitent attitude before God.

When we turn to Galatians, especially beginning with chapter three, the focus of Paul's arguments directed at the Galatian situation involves some disagreement about how one is recognized as truly a part of the family of Abraham. For Paul—and we will come back to this later—this happens by faith in Jesus Christ. But this is clearly not a traditional Jewish understanding of the importance of Abraham as forefather of a people. A more classic and popular Jewish conception would be that Abraham was the progenitor of a physical people group. Being a true part of that family involved association by birth and blood, marriage, or some type of conversion.[8] The promises of a great land for a great people were given to Abraham to share with his offspring. But who really *counts* as part of the people who stand to inherit this promise? This is where Paul makes a case that *gentiles* can have a share in this blessing even though they are ethnic outsiders. Their claim to this comes through Christ, and to

---

8. A number of early Jewish texts refer to Abraham as forefather for Israel (4Q176; 3 Macc 6:3; Josephus, *Ant.* 5.97, 113; *War* 4.531).

belong to Abraham means to live as Abraham did, by faith (hence Paul quoting Gen 15:6 and Hab 2:4).

I imagine the Jewish Christian rival teachers in Galatia making this argument to the gentile Galatian believers:

> You want to be a part of the Messiah's family? We welcome you with open arms. The gospel is good news for the whole world, and there is space for any and all in the Abrahamic family. But the pathway into this family is through officially entering the people of Israel, Abraham's ethnic children. And Abraham himself was the father of the covenant of circumcision. If you agree to circumcision, and obey the Law, you will find a family among us.

To be clear, I don't think these other teachers were anti-Messiah—they were preaching that Jesus is Messiah and Lord (as Paul did)—but they were *additionally* emphasizing the requirement of circumcision and works of the Law to secure their place in the Messiah's kingdom, heirs of the Abrahamic promise. If this situational reconstruction is accurate, then Paul was making the counter-case that gentile believers are welcome in the family, not by circumcision or works of the Law but by faith in Jesus only. Paul's arguments go down the following line of thought.

Abraham is not important as a physical father, but as a prototype of the true believer. Abraham *believed* God, and *that* was reckoned to him as righteousness; he was *justified* by his faith (3:6). Thus, when we look back at Abraham we ought not to focus on his flesh, but on his trust in God.

The promise of inheritance belongs to Abraham's destined "seed." While the promises and blessings given to Abraham were meant for him and his wider family, from Paul's perspective there is a special connection to his destined "seed," the Jewish

Messiah (3:16). Through this unique agent all nations (i.e., the gentiles) will be blessed (cf. 3:6–14). So, Paul sums up: "If you belong to Christ, then you are Abraham's offspring, heirs according to the promise" (3:29).

Isaac, Abraham's miracle child, is a symbol of God's promise and God's freedom; Ishmael represents slavery and flesh. Jews, like Paul, would have grown up hearing stories from their parents and grandparents about the ancestry line that split with Isaac and Ishmael. Paul reasons in 4:21–31 that there is a juxtaposition here, but it is ultimately not about narrowing the bloodline to Isaac. Rather, the inheritance that belongs to Isaac and those that come after him points toward freedom and abundance, which are found only in Christ, not in the flesh. Remember that Paul was concerned with the Galatian believers being manipulated into circumcision, but he did not have a concern with circumcision itself. He repeats in this letter that circumcision by itself does not make one closer to God, nor does it put him at a disadvantage (5:6; 6:15). The problem lies with the *value* one places on circumcision—is it a *requirement* for belonging to the people of God, the Abrahamic family? Paul argues that any attempt to force God's people into a flesh ritual is a sign of bondage rather than a symbol of Spirit and freedom. The allegorical nature of this passage can be hard to follow, and it is fruitless to try to make sense of all details. Paul's main point appears to be that there are two doors in front of the Galatians. One door is marked "true family," and the other is marked "slavery." The rival teachers believed that circumcision was a requirement to open the true family door. However, Paul warned the Galatians: if you are pressured into circumcision *as an obligation*, you might *think* you are opening a door to true family, but in fact you are locking yourself into the "slavery" choice.

ENTERING THROUGH THE SONSHIP OF JESUS

How exactly do gentiles become officially part of God's family? We
have mentioned that it is through faith in Jesus Christ, but
we can still say more. The way Paul explains this could be
called "united sonship." I am intentionally not using the word
"adoption," even though that term might seem natural here.
This is because modern Western adoption is not the same as
ancient adoption in the Greco-Roman world. But here I will
cite one of the key texts in Galatians about becoming family
where most translations do use the word "adoption" for the
Greek word *huiothesia*.

> But when the fullness of time had come, God sent his Son,
> born of a woman, born under the law, in order to redeem
> those who were under the law, so that we might receive
> *adoption as children* [*huiothesia*]. And because you are chil-
> dren [*huioi*, literally "sons"], God has sent the Spirit of his
> Son into our hearts, crying, "Abba! Father!" So you are no
> longer a slave but a child, and if a child then also an heir,
> through God. (4:4–7)

Paul is talking about moving people from a status of slave
and outsider to that of a "son" and insider. Using the English
word "adoption" does seem fitting (the closest modern analogy), but there are specifics in this passage and later in chapter four that really only make sense if we understand ancient
"sonship." There are four key ways that Roman "sonship" was
different from modern adoption.[9]

---

9. For a detailed discussion, see James C. Walters, "Paul, Adoption, and
Inheritance," in *Paul in the Greco-Roman World: A Handbook*, ed. J. Paul Sampley
(Harrisburg, PA: Trinity Press International, 2003), 42–76.

Men only. Only men were "adopted" in the Roman world, because that society's key concern was obtaining an heir when there was no male heir in the household. A patrimony (the family inheritance meant to be passed down from one generation to another) went through male heirs only, and the family name could only carry on through men. So, a man without a male child went through an official legal contract to create an heir. In Greek, this is called *huiothesia*, which literally means "positioned" (*thesia*) as a "son" (*huios*).

Practical, not benevolent. *Huiothesia* happened because a man needed a male heir, not because a family had compassion for an orphan. In modern times, typically people "down on their luck" are adopted. But that wasn't the case in Roman practice. In fact, a nobleman would be looking for someone of high status to become his selected heir.

Adults, not children. In modern practice, a family wanting to adopt generally desires a young child, perhaps even a baby. But in Roman *huiothesia* an heir is needed to take over when the *pater familias* (father) dies. Otherwise, the "son" is not yet needed. So, it was not unusual for adults to be "adopted" so that they could step in immediately after the father passed on.

Only one is needed. Another key element of *huiothesia* is that a family only really needs one male son. And in the case of no biological sons, only one adopted son is required. So, it would not make much sense for a family to adopt several boys. That is why I hesitate to call it "adoption." It is not about increasing a family; it is specifically about the legal need for a male heir to protect the family name and inheritance.

When we put all this together, we can see that Paul is using a specific focal image in his use of *huiothesia* in Galatians 4:4. The Son of God was sent to earth to rescue the unredeemed and give them the privilege of "sonship." But there is an assumption built into Paul's imagery that needs to be made explicit for modern readers. Only the unique Son of God has the special privilege of serving as the heir; Jesus is the only true "son" who deserves the inheritance. In any traditional family the oldest male would naturally be in a position of inheriting controlling power over the family, and sisters and other younger male siblings might naturally be jealous. What Paul makes clear about redeemed sinners as children of God is that they *all* become equal and true heirs along with Jesus the Son. But how? This is what I call "united sonship." Believers become one with Jesus the Son by faith and have a share in his unique sonship. Thus, the Spirit makes a direct link from believer to *Abba* Father through the sonship of Jesus. We see this "theological logic" present in Romans 8:29, where Paul explains that the Son of God came to earth so that he might be "the firstborn within a large family" (in Greek, literally, "firstborn among many brothers and sisters").

This brings clarity to some of the language Paul uses in Galatians 4. First, believers are not just "adopted" (in the modern sense), but are incorporated into the unique sonship of Jesus (*huiothesia*). Second, they are not just "children of God" in a general sense, but all (both men and women) are treated as "sons" (*huioi*). This is not Paul preferencing male language as if he were a misogynist. Rather, he was demonstrating that even women have an equal claim to inheriting the kingdom of God.

This sheds fresh light on the famous Gal 3:28 statement, "there is no longer male and female." Paul was not dismissing the phenomena of sex and gender in general. He was making a specific statement about access to the privilege of being a true child of God and a *bona fide* heir. There are no tiers of importance or value; what matters is only whether one belongs to Jesus the Son—believers find their status, privilege, and worth by union with him. In the wider passage (3:22–29), Paul's main point is that Jewish Law played a specific and limited role until the coming of the Messiah. Through the Messiah, the Son of God, Jews and gentiles both become children (literally, in Greek, "sons" [*huioi*]) by faith. The process is baptism and clothing themselves in Christ Jesus, taking his status in the family as their own. Any and all who are immersed in Jesus the Son are not sized up based on ethnicity, status, or gender, but all are one by association with Jesus. By faith they become part of the family of Abraham, "heirs according to the promise" (3:29).

The idea of united sonship is reinforced by what Paul writes in 2:19–20:

> I have been crucified with Christ; and it is no longer I who live, but it is Christ who lives in me. And the life I now live in the flesh I live by faith in the Son of God, who loved me and gave himself for me.

Dying with Christ is a prerequisite for living in Christ. Life, then, is united with the Son of God. This is the entry point to experiencing and knowing God. It is the living connection to God's family (again, pay special attention to the language of "Son of God" here).

BELOVED BROTHERS AND SISTERS THROUGH GOD'S SON

If it is true that "adoption" (*huiothesia*) takes place through the unique position of the Son of God, i.e., "united sonship," then it stands to reason that believers will treat each other as family, as brothers and sisters. No wonder, then, that Paul repeatedly uses familial language for Christian belonging. He often calls believers "my brothers and sisters," and this language is noticeable in Galatians, which is especially pre-occupied with family imagery.

Before digging into Galatians, we can address a common question about Paul's siblingship language: when he talks about Christian "brothers," is he intentionally referencing men to the exclusion of women? One *might* get that impression based on the fact that Paul uses the grammatically masculine word *adelphos* (and does not use the feminine counterpart *adelphe⁻*, which means "sister"). But two things need to be said about this. First, it was extremely common in Koine Greek for writers and speakers to use a grammatically masculine term for a general category that may include women. For example, in English we might address a room as "Hey guys!" without trying to exclude women. Secondly, there are times where we can simply assume women were in the room when Paul's letters were read to the recipients. For instance, in his letter to the Romans Paul uses *adelphoi* ("my brothers") repeatedly throughout, but Rom 16:3–16 clearly indicates that a num-ber of Christian women would have been present since they are acknowledged in that passage. So, when Paul uses the vocative[10] plural form of *adelphos*, *adelphoi*, it is accurate to translate this "brothers and sisters."

Here's a quick breakdown of how sibling language is used by Paul in Galatians: Paul writes to the Galatians and sends greetings from the "brothers and sisters" who are with him (1:2)—probably to show universal solidarity in the household of God. Paul was not a "fringe" apostle, gaining notoriety in

---

10. The Greek vocative form is the "naming" designation, when a writer/speaker calls out directly to someone.

a particular territory; his ministry was a vocation focused on gentiles wherever they were in the world. Paul also tends to call the Galatians his "brothers and sisters" when he makes a serious point; for example, when he strongly asserts the authenticity of his gospel message (1:11; cf. also 3:15; 4:12, 28; 5:11, 13; 6:1). In one of Paul's most urgent statements in the letter, he writes, "So then, brothers and sisters (*adelphoi*), we are children, not of an enslaved woman but of the free woman. For freedom Christ has set us free. Stand firm, therefore, and do not submit again to a yoke of slavery" (4:31–5:1).[11]

Paul calls out certain troublemakers as "false brothers," who pretend to have "family" interests in mind but do not have the genuine marks of true Christian kinship (2:4), pure faith in Christ alone. And the very last words of Galatians serve as a bookend to this sibling imagery: "May the grace of our Lord Jesus Christ be with your spirit, brothers and sisters. Amen" (6:18).

Before we can fully appreciate the theological significance of this siblingship imagery for Paul, we need to understand the sibling relationship in ancient families. Siblings, brothers and sisters, formed one of the strongest relational bonds in the Greco-Roman family.[12] Aristotle, for example, argued that this bond is even stronger than that of a husband-wife, since biological siblings have shared memories and life experiences from childhood onward (*Nic. Eth.* 8.1.12.3). Paul probably drew from this wider siblingship ethos as he conceived of a "Christian" family community. David deSilva identifies four virtues of the sibling relationship as we look at how people in Paul's time thought about the makeup of a healthy family:

---

11. NRSVue. The NRSV preferred to translate *adelphoi* as "friends," while the NRSVue (updated edition) changed it to "brothers and sisters," the update (thankfully!) retaining the Pauline metaphor.

12. deSilva, *Honor, Patronage, Kinship, and Purity*, 189.

Cooperation, Not Competition. While people, in general, saw others as competitors for honor, family was "off-limits." You never wanted to shame your own family (unless you were going to excommunicate family members for engaging in taboo behaviors). Brothers and sisters naturally saw themselves as one team seeking to pool honor for their whole family and to increase their collective reputation *together.*

Trust. Siblings could let their guard down with family; they could be vulnerable with and open up to each other. They leaned on one another for support.

Harmony: Sharing Ideals and Possessions. Because a family wanted to show unity in life and community, it makes sense that brothers and sisters would be comfortable sharing money and possessions. The famous parable of the prodigal son shows the tension of an older brother jealous of the lavish generosity of the father toward the "prodigal," but it also highlights the father's emphasis: "Son, you are always with me, and all that is mine is yours" (Luke 15:31).

Longsuffering. Conflict among family members is inevitable; we know that brothers and sisters fight and hurt each other's feelings. But the ideal family shows patience and longsuffering; family members do not harbor a permanent grudge, ignore the other, or take revenge. While there are many famous stories of "sibling rivalries" ancient and modern, the healthy family cherishes the other enough to want to repair a broken relationship.

To what degree Paul had all these things in mind when he used sibling language is not entirely clear. But what we can say for sure is that Paul wanted fellow Christians to see each other and treat each other as *family*, and this is all the more urgent in Galatians where the most contentious issues seem to be how gentiles are considered part of the family of (Israel's) God and what level of inclusion is appropriate for them. Paul makes no qualifications, considering all believers to be full and true members of the great household of God. In Roman households, truth be told, you had tiers of importance—the *pater familias* was the head, of course, but the wife, the woman of the house, was also significant. The eldest biological son of the household was prime heir and as an adult was a leader in the family. Other household members would have varying levels of influence and importance based on status, biology, age, and gender. Children were not very significant until they came of age (4:1–3). Slaves were not true family members at all, but more like pets or work animals—property rather than bona fide community members. It was not uncommon for the *pater familias* to have sex with some of his female slaves and for children to be born from these women. What, then, of those children? What status did they have in the household? By birth, they were slaves (born of a slave); the *pater familias* in practice *could* treat that child as a son, offering warmth, advice, and even respect. But in the eyes of Roman law and the customs of Roman culture, that slave-born son would never be equal to his half-siblings who were not slave-born. Nevertheless, Paul explains that in the household of God there are no privileged and unprivileged sons or daughters, and thus all brothers and sisters are on the same footing *because* of Jesus Christ the Son who graciously shares his status and privilege with anyone who proudly wears his name (3:27–29). Christ freely opens up his Sonship to all without discrimination. Because of this, Jesus the Son creates a non-competitive environment for the household; brothers and sisters ought not to fight with one another for the attention of the Father, for glory or fame, or for resources.

Galatians 6:1–4 offers a set of ideal dynamics of the Christian community as a loving family. Paul warns these *adelphoi* (brothers and sisters) that when they discover some-one in sin, the Spirit ought to guide believers to handle the matter with *gentleness* (versus mockery, derision, or conceit). Now is not the time to wrestle with the interpretive challenges of Paul's "law of Christ" language in 6:2, but one way to take this is as some kind of household ethos—*what guides how Christian brothers and sisters live together?* Paul does make clear the driving virtue of this ethos (or "law" [*nomos*]): love. Love is expressed in terms of bearing one another's burdens. Paul addresses this in 5:14 when he explains that the whole of the Jewish Law can be summed up in the biblical commandment "You shall love your neighbor as yourself."

We have commenced our study of the main themes of Galatians with the family and household imagery because it is both a pervasive part of Paul's letter and is seriously neglected in the study of Galatians. It is tempting to begin with "justifi-cation" because of the heated debates since the Reformation period on the nature of *dikaiosyne* (justification/righteous-ness) and *dikaioō* ("to justify/make right[eous]") in Pauline theology. But, truth be told, Paul's justification language is concentrated in chapters two and three of Galatians, while family language is present and prominent from the beginning to the end of the letter. Put another way, the main question Paul addresses in Galatians is *not*: "How is a gentile justi-fied?" Yes, Paul does try to answer that question, especially in 2:16–3:24, but more broadly he addresses the question: "How does one become a *bona fide* part of God's family?" And the answer, for both Jew and gentile, is: through the one Son of God, Jesus Christ. All die (as Paul did) by being crucified with Christ, all have the opportunity for Christ to come alive in them, and all must then live by faith in the Son of God who loved sinners and gave his life for them (2:19–20). As a result, all obtain the privilege of being brothers and sisters of the Messiah Son, children of *Abba* Father, and equal co-heirs of the Abrahamic promise and eternal inheritance.

SUGGESTED READING

Aasgaard, Reidar. *"My Beloved Brothers and Sisters!" Christian Siblingship in Paul.* London: T&T Clark, 2004.

Barton, Stephen C., ed. *The Family in Theological Perspective.* Edinburgh: T&T Clark, 1996.

deSilva, David. *Honor, Patronage, Kinship, and Purity: Unlocking New Testament Culture.* 2nd ed. Downers Grove: IVP Academic, 2022.

Hellerman, Joseph H. *The Ancient Church as Family.* Minneapolis: Fortress Press, 2001.

———. *When the Church Was a Family: Recapturing Jesus' Vision for Authentic Christian Community.* Nashville: B&H Academic, 2009.

McKnight, Scot. *Pastor Paul: Nurturing a Culture of Christoformity in the Church.* Grand Rapids: Brazos Press, 2019. See chapter 3: "A Culture of Siblings."

Trebilco, Paul. *Self-Designations and Group Identity in the New Testament.* Cambridge: Cambridge University Press, 2012. See chapter 2: "Brothers and Sisters—ἀδελφοί."

CHAPTER 4

Faith: Knowing God through Participation in Jesus Christ

Wlhen we use the language of "faith traditions" or "state-ment of faith" as a way of talking about religion, there is no getting around the fact that this is distinctly *Christian* language. Christianity is a *creedal* religion, emphasizing the essential nature of beliefs. In fact, the word "creed" comes from the Latin *credo*, "I believe." As early as the middle of the first century CE, Christians called each other "believers" and referred to outsiders as "unbelievers." The Apostles' Creed probably dates back to the second or third century, as believers sought unity of belief and confession for the church.[1]

The Christian emphasis on faith has something to do with the teaching of Jesus, of course. Jesus himself called for repentance and *faith* in the good news he was preaching (Mark 1:14–15). Jesus commended the faith of those who followed him, chastised his Twelve for having too little faith, and claimed that true faith even in small amounts could move great mountains. But faith language is most distinc-tive in the writings of Paul.[2] Although the Greek words *pistis*

---

1. See Luke Timothy Johnson, *The Creed: What Christians Believe and Why It Matters* (New York: Doubleday, 2003).
2. For an expanded discussion, see Nijay K. Gupta, *Paul and the Language of Faith* (Grand Rapids: Eerdmans, 2020).

(faith) and *pisteuō* (believe) appear in highest frequency in the lengthy letter to the Romans, Paul's conception of "faith" is most powerfully expressed in Galatians, and therefore is of special thematic interest for a few reasons. First, most scholars agree that Galatians is one of Paul's earliest extant letters, if not *the* earliest, so we might be witnessing Paul working out his theology of faith right here. Second, Galatians is a text articulating the fundamentals of the gospel in the midst of ongoing debates and disagreements in the early church. Paul was pressed to make the true gospel crystal clear, and therefore key agenda-setting statements are made in this potent text. Third, Galatians is a text where Paul includes important narrative reflections on historical events, such as his own conversion (for lack of a better term) and crucial conversations with Jerusalem leadership. Finally, Paul engages with formative faith language in the Scriptures, such as the belief of Abraham (Gen 15:6; Gal 3:6–9) and the essential nature of covenantal "faith" in Habakkuk 2:4 ("the one who is righteous will live by faith"; Gal 3:11).

One of the challenges with identifying "faith" as a key theme in Galatians is overcoming some of the misleading assumptions we have about faith language in the Bible. I want to mention three of these here to quickly get them out of the way:

Myth 1: Faith as Passive. It is somewhat common to hear modern Christians talk about faith as the opposite of works, specifically using a type of relinquishment phenomenon—*let go and let God*. I imagine this sentiment draws from Paul's repeated emphasis on faith in Christ over and against "works of the Law," a juxtaposition classically expressed in Galatians 2:16–17. But the Greek language of *pistis* (often translated "faith"

in English Bibles) does not fit that notion of passivity
or nonaction. In fact, biblical writers could talk about
doing or *performing* faith (Matt 23:23), and in Galatians
Paul refers to "faith *working* through love" (5:6). Paul
was, indeed, drawing a line of difference between
believing/having faith and doing works of the Law,
but this was never meant to be reduced to believing vs.
doing. After all, Paul was insistent that the Galatians
do certain things and *not do* other things (5:13–6:16)!

Myth 2: Faith as Doctrine. Another misleading idea is that
faith primarily refers to doctrine, as in "faith statement." Now, at times Paul did note how one aspect of
faith is what the mind believes (2 Cor 5:7). The mind
plays a dominant role in directing action. In that
sense, faith requires correct belief. But it is dangerous
and problematic to equate faith with doctrine, especially if what we mean by doctrine is a list of beliefs on
a mental checklist. For Paul, *pistis* (faith) was a multi-
dimensional phenomenon that included belief, will,
and the orientation of the whole being. Faith involves
tethering the deepest part of self to another person
or thing. It is a whole-self dynamic that goes beyond
learning about and assenting to certain beliefs.

Myth 3: Faith as Anti-Reason. Finally, sometimes modern faith discourse can be used to imply that faith
is anti-reason or anti-logic. For example, someone
might say, "I can't prove God exists, or that Jesus rose
from the dead, I just believe it by faith." This person is claiming that "faith" is a way of talking about
unsubstantiated or unprovable opinions. But that's
not actually how Paul refers to faith. Faith may involve
something hard to perceive through natural senses,
but it is not unreasonable or just a feeling, opinion,

or hunch. For example, Paul was an intellectual in his own right, writing sometimes very long letters (like 1 Corinthians) and offering sophisticated arguments and proofs to back up his thoughts. He may have called for faith that was difficult or sometimes countercultural or counterintuitive, but his defense of faith was never baseless or without reason.

So, what exactly *is* "faith" as Paul saw it? We will be diving deeper into that question in a moment, but it is worth noticing that sometimes early Christians could use *pistis* to represent the whole package of religion, commitment, lifestyle, belief, and action—something like a technical term for Christianity itself. We see this in Galatians, in fact, when Paul recounts how Christians initially reacted to his newfound allegiance to Jesus Christ.

> Then I went into the regions of Syria and Cilicia, and I was still unknown by sight to the churches of Judea that are in Christ; they only heard it said, "The one who formerly was persecuting us is now proclaiming the **faith** [*pistis*] he once tried to destroy." And they glorified God because of me. (1:21–24)

Here, when Paul refers to his 180-degree turn on Jesus, he uses the language of preaching the "faith" (*pistis*) that he used to oppose. "Faith," here, is not just a set of religious beliefs, though surely Paul had beliefs about Jesus in mind as a part of the whole. Paul the zealous and persecuting Pharisee was not simply trying to refute a set of beliefs, but rather was resisting a whole movement: a people with distinctive ideas about the divine, a large following, with regional communities, and a whole way of living. "Faith" here is used as a catch-all term for the whole of Christianity: Messiah, people, beliefs, and the kitchen sink.[3]

This is just one way that New Testament writers like Paul could use a very elastic term (*pistis*). "Faith" became such an important word for Christianity that it took on a life of its own and became difficult to pin down to just one meaning. We will showcase the range of connotations and nuances that *pistis* has in Galatians, but an important place to begin is the way Paul uses faith language as a distinctive mark of his true gospel, especially in chapters two and three where he sets up a contrast between "faith in Jesus Christ" and "works of the Law."

THE WAY OF WORKS OF THE LAW, AND THE WAY OF FAITH IN CHRIST JESUS *ALONE*

In my book *Paul and the Language of Faith*, I present a theory about how to interpret Paul's faith language in Galatians, especially this contrast between "faith in Jesus Christ" and "works of the Law" (2:16–17). Throughout the centuries, some interpreters have tried to articulate and defend a perspective that Paul was promoting faith (as something essentially internal and passive) and repudiating works *as* works (i.e., legalism and "doing" something for God, meritorious works). The problem with this approach, as we have already explained, is that biblical writers (including Paul) were often quite comfortable seeing "faith" as something that the believer *does* (e.g., 5:6). There was no inherent disjunction between believing and doing. And there is, in fact, a serious problem with emphasizing "faith" to the *exclusion* of "works," as explained in the book of James:

---

3. Other examples of this all-encompassing use of *pistis* might include Acts 6:7; 13:8; 14:22; Phil 1:27; 1 Tim 3:9; 4:1; 6:12.

What good is it, my brothers and sisters, if you say you have faith but do not have works? Can faith save you? If a brother or sister is naked and lacks daily food, and one of you says to them, "Go in peace; keep warm and eat your fill," and yet you do not supply their bodily needs, what is the good of that? So faith by itself, if it has no works, is dead.

But someone will say, "You have faith and I have works." Show me your faith apart from your works, and I by my works will show you my faith. You believe that God is one; you do well. Even the demons believe—and shudder. Do you want to be shown, you senseless person, that faith apart from works is barren? Was not our ancestor Abraham justified by works when he offered his son Isaac on the altar? You see that faith was active along with his works, and faith was brought to completion by the works. Thus the scripture was fulfilled that says, "Abraham believed God, and it was reckoned to him as righteousness," and he was called the friend of God. You see that a person is justified by works and not by faith alone. Likewise, was not Rahab the prostitute also justified by works when she welcomed the messengers and sent them out by another road? For just as the body without the spirit is dead, so faith without works is also dead. (James 2:14–26)

James is probably responding to some false teaching that makes too sharp of a distinction between faith and works, placing premium value on the former and ignoring the latter. James treats this teaching as hypocritical and ineffectual. In fact, Abraham, the great patriarch, was justified by his *works*, as his actions were a natural outworking of his faith (James 2:21). James argues that both faith *and* works lead to being right with God, not faith alone. When you put Galatians

chapter two side by side with James chapter two, it is easy to
jump to conclusions and read James as a refutation of Paul,
and of Galatians in particular. I don't think that is what is
going on, because I think Paul would actually *agree* with
James! Here is one key difference when you compare these two
texts: Paul emphasizes that justification cannot come through
works *of the Law*, but James does not mention the Jewish Law
at all in his passage. What I think is behind the James text is
a reaction, not to Paul, but to followers of Paul ("Paulinists")
who had misread him and took his theology in the wrong
direction. Paul, again, was not saying mental faith is all that is
necessary, and he was also not saying works were unnecessary.
He was rather addressing a specific false teaching—"another
gospel"—that was being taught to the Galatians by certain
outsiders. Paul wrote his letter to the Galatians to clarify the
nature of the true gospel. I will now offer my understanding
of Paul's train of thought in context, and if you want all the
details, footnotes, and more thorough argumentation, see my
chapter on Galatians in *Paul and the Language of Faith*.

Let's begin with 2:15–21, because this is the beginning of
Paul's faith/law discussion in the letter:

> We ourselves are Jews by birth and not Gentile sinners; yet
> we know that a person is justified not by the works of the
> law but through faith in Jesus Christ. And we have come to
> believe in Christ Jesus, so that we might be justified by faith
> in Christ, and not by doing the works of the law, because
> no one will be justified by the works of the law. But if,
> in our effort to be justified in Christ, we ourselves have
> been found to be sinners, is Christ then a servant of sin?
> Certainly not! But if I build up again the very things that I
> once tore down, then I demonstrate that I am a transgres-
> sor. For through the law I died to the law, so that I might

live to God. I have been crucified with Christ; and it is no longer I who live, but it is Christ who lives in me. And the life I now live in the flesh I live by faith in the Son of God, who loved me and gave himself for me. I do not nullify the grace of God; for if justification comes through the law, then Christ died for nothing.

On the surface, it might appear that Paul and the rival teachers in Galatia are represented in the not/but statements in 2:16–17:

Traditional Approach to Paul vs. His Rivals
Paul: justification by faith in Jesus Christ
Rivals: justification by works of the Law

But there is a problem with this approach—it doesn't take into account that Jews in this time period were already comfortable talking about their Jewish religion and piety in terms of "faith." The Jewish historian Josephus, for example, sometimes used *pistis* in the plural to talk about the Jewish covenant, which could be translated as "mutual pledges of fidelity."[4] In the Septuagint (Greek Old Testament) version of Nehemiah 10:1, the Israelite leaders who began to rebuild the temple made a covenantal oath to be faithful to God, and the language used is *pistis* (covenantal fidelity). In the New Testament, Jesus calls out the Pharisees for neglecting the weightier matters of the Law such as justice (*krisis*), mercy (*eleos*), and faith/faithfulness (*pistis*) (Matt 23:23). Jesus was reminding the Pharisees of their covenantal obligation of true commitment and faithfulness to God; *pistis* is built into Israel's religion.

---

4. See Josephus, *Antiquities* 6.234, 276, 291; 7.361; 8.334; 10.2.

So, if the rival teachers in Galatia were Jewish Christians (which is a common assumption by scholars), it makes sense that they believed and preached justification by faith in God and God's Messiah Jesus. But, given their emphasis on the Law, it is probable that they preached justification by faith in Christ *through* performing works of the Law. Just as we saw in James, works could be seen as the demonstration of faith, the living out of what is inside. But these rival teachers in Galatians were specifically focused on performing Jewish covenantal rituals such as circumcision. They clearly saw these "works of the Law" as necessary demonstrations of Christian faith for Jews *and* for gentiles. So, the unique part of Paul's teaching is actually *not* his inclusion of "faith," but rather his exclusion of "works of the Law" (and thus his *sole* emphasis on "faith"). Therefore, we might lay out the two views in this way:

Gupta's Approach to Paul vs. His Rivals
Rivals: justification by faith in Jesus Christ through works of the Law

Paul: justification by faith in Jesus Christ (alone)

Now those of us today (post-Reformation) who are familiar with the doctrine *sola fide* ("by faith alone") might not find what Paul says as striking or radical. He was just sharing the essence of Christianity, wasn't he? But when Paul wrote Galatians, he was taking "works of the Law" out of the equation of Christianity. This would have been a radical move in the eyes of many of his Christian peers, especially fellow Jews who emphasized a central role for the Jewish Law in their worship of God. We can easily turn to Acts 15 to see the heated conversations among Jewish leaders about whether Christians are expected to perform the works of the Jewish Law. Some teachers claimed, "Unless you are circumcised according to the custom of Moses, you cannot be saved" (Acts 15:1); similarly, others required keeping the Law of Moses (15:5). This raised questions and stirred debate. Peter then pronounced to them that salvation is only by the grace of God, without additional requirement (Acts 15:11). We today know this was the inevitable outcome, but we have to think about how jarring it would have been to the majority of the apostles and the leaders of Jewish Christian communities. God had given his people, Israel, the Law of Moses as a gift, a compass and manual to guide their collective lives. This Law had done so for hundreds of years. Many Jewish Christians would have simply taken for granted that believers in the Messiah, whether Jews or gentiles, ought to demonstrate their faith and fidelity *through* obeying and keeping the holy Law of God.

In Galatians, Paul articulates, perhaps for the first time in extended written argumentation, how a right relationship with God necessitates only "faith in Jesus Christ" without the requirement of practicing works of the Law. While it was natural for some (like the rival teachers) to see performing works of the Law as *the* practical piety of this "faith," Paul separated these works from faith. Paul did not do this because he was against the Jewish Law per se, but because he believed that a deeper and wholehearted personal commitment to Jesus was the *only* thing that was necessary. To add anything else—even commandments of the Law—as a *requirement* would inevitably conflict with this primary Christ-oriented relationship. Paul was not *against* the Law or carrying out commands written in the Law; there is much in the Law to commend (such as the holy commandments to love one's neighbor; 5:14). Brian Rosner has made the case that while Paul did not *reject* the Law as he put his faith in Christ, he did reorient himself to the Law. It no longer played the role of requiring him to live out his piety in a specific way; rather, it became a prime source of wisdom that guided him in living out his faith in Christ.[5]

THE "FAITH OF CHRIST" DEBATE

Before we move on in our discussion of Galatians 2–3, there is an academic "elephant in the room" that I want to address. (Not all readers will know this elephant exists, so just watch where you step after you read the following explanation.) Paul repeats a phrase in Galatians (and other letters like Romans) that can be interpreted in different ways. The Greek phrase *pistis Christou* can be woodenly translated as "faith of Christ."[6] The relationship between these two Greek words is ambiguous.[7] There are many possible ways of looking at the meaning of this phrase, but two readings have dominated. One view can be called the "Christ" interpretation, which refers to the *faithfulness* demonstrated by Christ himself.[8] If we look at Galatians 2:16, this is, in fact, the preferred reading we find in the NET translation:

> . . . so that we may be justified by the faithfulness of Christ and not by the works of the law.

---

5. Brian S. Rosner, *Paul and the Law: Keeping the Commandments of God* (Downers Grove: IVP Academic, 2013).

6. A common variation is *pistis Iēsou Christou*, "faith of Jesus Christ."

7. This is called a genitive case syntactical construction, with *Christou* in the genitive noun case and *pistis* as the head noun. The genitive case signals some kind of relationship, but the nature of that relationship is determined by context. For a more thorough discussion of the state of the academic discussion, see Nijay K. Gupta, "Paul and *Pistis Christou*," in *The Oxford Handbook of Pauline Studies*, ed. Matthew V. Novenson and R. Barry Matlock (Oxford: Oxford University Press, 2022), 470–87.

8. In scholarship this is called the "subjective genitive" interpretation, because in the Greek construction *pistis* is viewed as a "verbal noun" (representing an action) and *Christou* is seen as indicating the subject of the action.

In this case, believers are justified, not by their own "faith" but by Christ's faithfulness—either his faith and obedience toward God or his faithfulness toward sinful humanity, or both. While this view is currently in the minority among modern English translations of the Bible, it has prominent support among many Pauline scholars.[9]

The second view could be called the "believer" interpretation, and in this case *pistis* is understood as the faith of the Christian. This approach is taken by many English translations, as we just noted, and the NIV offers a clear example for Galatians 2:16:

> . . . a person is not justified by the works of the law, but by faith in Jesus Christ.

Here the focus is on the faith of the believer. Believers are not justified by themselves; faith is not treated as a saving action, but rather the means by which believers are rectified by Christ's atoning death. Space does not permit an extensive discussion of this debate, which has an ever-expanding library of scholarship. It suffices to say that scholars are in a bit of a stalemate on this debate; evidence has been put forward in favor of both sides, as well as counterarguments. Most scholars will agree that, regardless of exactly how *pistis Christou* should be interpreted, in general Paul emphasizes *both* the unique saving work of Christ *and* necessity of belief.

There are also a number of "third option" approaches that try to add something new to the conversation. Personally, I favor a "third option" because there is no easy way to prove one or the other readings just explained. Paul was possibly

---

9. See Richard B. Hays, *The Faith of Jesus Christ: The Narrative Substructure of Galatians 3:1–4:11*, 2nd ed. (Grand Rapids: Eerdmans, 2002).

not trying to express something very specific about Christ's faithfulness *or* human faith in Christ, but rather was trying to talk about (what I call) "the Christ relation" in a holistic way without putting the emphasis on just one side. In that case, Paul was pointing to justification happening in light of all that Christ brings to the whole scene, as a new kind of mediator between God and his people. The emphasis, then, would be on the new kind or version of a relationship with God, not on exactly who is doing what and how justification works on a mechanical level. Even though I favor a third approach, I find the "believer" interpretation more likely than the "Christ" interpretation, if I had to choose between the two most popular options. So that the discussion of "faith" in the rest of this chapter doesn't get too convoluted, I will default to the "believer" reading whenever it is relevant to the discussion.

ABRAHAM AND FAITH

For the rest of this chapter, our focus will be on different facets of Paul's faith language in Galatians. Starting in 3:6, Paul introduces the patriarch Abraham into the discussion. First, he questions the Galatian believers who are buying into the arguments of the rivals: "Did you receive the Spirit by doing the works of the law or by believing what you heard? Are you so foolish? Having started with the Spirit, are you now ending with the flesh? . . . [D]oes God supply you with the Spirit and work miracles among you by your doing the works of the law, or by your believing what you heard?" (3:2–3, 5). Paul thus presents a clear either-or binary when it comes to the Galatians' religious orientation. Either the catalyzing factor is faith or it is performing works of the Law. In Paul's mind, it can't be both. After this series of rhetorical questions, he abruptly quotes Genesis 15:6: Abraham "believed

God, and it was reckoned to him as righteousness" (Gal 3:6). This proves, for Paul, the point that the people of God demonstrate their association with Abraham not by blood or conversion ritual (i.e., circumcision), but by *believing*, just as Abraham believed.

It is probably not the case that Paul just happened to come up with an Abraham argument in this text. Many scholars believe that the *rivals* had first introduced Abraham into the conversation (when they were in Galatia), and in this letter Paul was offering a counterargument looking at Abraham in another way. Because it is clear enough that the rivals were pressuring the Galatian men to be circumcised (5:3), it is also fathomable that these teachers supported this recommendation by appealing to the first patriarch and the institution of circumcision as a covenantal obligation (Gen 17:1–14). They may have tried to impress upon Galatian gentiles an argument like this:

> **Rivals:** If you want to be part of Abraham's family, Israel, then you need to join the Abrahamic covenant in an official way—through circumcision, the gateway ritual of conversion.

For example, Philo of Alexandra during the first century CE answers the question that readers might ask: *Why did Abraham circumcise foreigners?* Philo's answer is this: the consecration of the self through circumcision leads to self-control and pure devotion to God. Any gentile wanting to live with self-mastery is wise to adopt the Jewish ritual of circumcision associated with Abraham, the Jewish patriarch (Philo, *Genesis* 3.62). However, Paul, on the basis of reading the Old Testament through the lens of Jesus Christ, identifies Abraham with *faith*, not circumcision per se. The true descendants[10] of Abraham, then, are *hoi ek pisteōs* (3:7); this phrase is sometimes translated "those who believe," although a more literal rendering would be "those by [means of] faith." In the next verse, Paul refers to Scripture's testimony (in the Abraham story) that gentiles would be justified *ek pisteōs*, "by [means of] faith." Understanding these precise details of wording is important, because it is clear in Greek that Paul is setting up a "this-not-that." Justification—becoming right with God, becoming a true part of God's family—comes not as a result of circumcision, but *by faith only*. So, Christians are *by-faith* people, just like Abraham was a *by-faith* person.

This leads to a natural set of questions: *What does "faith" mean for Paul in this situation (3:6–9)? What about Abraham's belief is meant to be a type or model for Christian faith?* If you turn back to Genesis 15, it is clear that we are not talking about "beliefs" like atonement or the Trinity. Genesis 15 begins with Abraham worrying about the future of his family. He was without a legitimate heir and, having recently waged war, he was also low on resources. At this point, God shows Abraham the bright starry sky and promises him countless descendants like the multitude of celestial lights. The Lord brought Abraham out of the safety of his homeland (Ur of the Chaldeans) and promised that he would have a fertile new land of his own. These weren't invisible or "spiritual" promises; these were tangible things (people and land), and Abraham took great risks of resources, time, and relationships to follow these directions from God. So, Abraham's willingness to enter into a covenant with this God required "belief" that is personal, communal, practical, and comprehensive. Abraham was entrusting all that he was, and all that he had, in partnership

---

10. In Greek, the word used here is *huioi*, "sons," referring to descendants who are heirs.

with this strange God who promised him a hope and a future far away from everything he knew and all the securities he had in his ancestral land. For Abraham, as for the *by-faithers* after him, "faith" was a deep relational trust that what God has done proves his intentions, and what he has promised for the future can be treated as reliable and real.

It is worth exploring briefly one more curiosity related to faith in the Abrahamic discourses in Galatians. Paul concludes his first section on Abraham (3:6–9) with this phrase: *hōste hoi ek pisteōs eulogountai syn to pistō Abraam.* We can translate it in a wooden and literal way as: "So then, the by-faithers are blessed along with [*pistō*] Abraham." I want to focus on the meaning of the word *pistō*[11] here. The adjective *pistos* means "faithful," and that is how it is translated in the vast majority of cases in the Greek Bible. However, most English translations of 3:9 translate *pistos* using some form of "belief" language:

NET: "Abraham the believer"
NIV/ESV: "Abraham, the man of faith"
CEB: "Abraham who believed"
CSB: "Abraham, who had faith"

However, a more natural reading of Paul's use of *pistos* as an adjective modifying a noun is "faithful Abraham," as we find in the KJV: "So then they which be of faith are blessed with *faithful Abraham.*" If Paul had wanted to refer to "Abraham who believed" in a clear way, he would have used a verb (in Greek, a participle in particular) focusing on the activity of faith, or simply repeated *ek pisteōs* ("by faith"). By using an adjective (*pistos*) that tends to involve a social virtue

---

11. *Pistō* is a form (masculine dative singular) of the adjective *pistos.*

(fidelity, loyalty), it is unlikely Paul was referring to belief. So, why do these modern translations prefer belief/faith language for *pistos* here? The flow of 3:6–9 is precisely meant to argue that Christians are connected to Abraham's family *not by works of the Law like circumcision*, but by faith (*ek pisteōs*). However, right here at the end of the section, Paul chooses *pistos* ("faithful") to describe Abraham rather than *ek pisteōs*.

What was Paul doing? I think he was making a point about the nature of faith. On the one hand, we can separate faith and works, just like we can distinguish thought from action. So Paul can, in theory, emphasize Abraham's *faith* as what God deemed as righteousness, not Abraham's works (like circumcision). And *yet* faith and action go hand in hand—it is very difficult to hit the pause button on the *exact* moment when faith becomes action. I think Paul is saying here that although Abraham is rightly the model of *faith*, he is also a model of *faithfulness*. While righteousness is reckoned on the basis of faith (before and apart from works), true faith becomes faithfulness—the activity of faith leads to action. This is Paul's way of being careful not to present "faith" as something merely cognitive or intangible. Abraham the believer *is also* "faithful Abraham." He is a guide in *both* faith and obedience. If we interpret Galatians 3:9 the way I am suggesting, this closes the (perceived) gap a bit between Galatians 2 (Paul's faith/works dichotomy) and James 2 (James's faith and works emphasis).

"THE ONE WHO IS RIGHTEOUS WILL LIVE BY FAITH" (HAB 2:4; GAL 3:11)

In the section of Galatians following the first Abrahamic discourse, Paul presents two different religious paths. One is *ek pisteōs*, which was the point of focus of 3:6–9, the way of faith associated with Abraham who believed the promises of God. Starting with 3:10, Paul makes reference to those people who are *eks ergōn nomou* (lit. "from works of the Law").[12] One path is faith and the other is works of the Law—door number one and door number two. But door number two leads to a curse (3:10b). One door alone leads to being right before God, and in Paul's mind no one can have it both ways. One door ends with rejection and damnation, but the other is the true route to belonging and salvation. One of the ways that Paul discounts works of the Law as a path to justification is by appealing to Hab 2:4: "The one who is righteous will live by faith" (Gal 3:11). We will get to the context of Habakkuk in a moment. For now, I want to track Paul's line of reasoning. He appears to be saying this: *Habakkuk 2:4 tells us that faith is the only way of life for the righteous, so keeping the works of the Law is not the correct path to take. If someone chooses to follow the Law's way, it leads to a dead end (a curse).*

It is important to make some clarifications here about what Paul is (and is not) talking about in relation to works of the Law. First, he is not talking about whether or not Christians should do good works. Paul takes this for granted (Gal 5:22–23; cf. Eph 2:9–10). He is also not talking about completely discarding the Old Testament. In fact, in Paul's attempt to turn the Galatians toward faith and away from the Law, he *quotes* the Jewish Scriptures, assuming their ongoing authority and prophetic testimony for the present time. When Paul repudiates the way of "works of the Law," he is referring to a whole framework of understanding one's relationship with God and what it means to be counted as in a right relationship with God—to be justified. The Law

---

12. The *ek* from *ek pisteōs* and the *eks* from *eks ergōn nomou* are essentially the same Greek preposition meaning "from/by."

can play a positive role in shaping Christian behavior, but it cannot be treated as the *sine qua non* for justification. Now let's turn to Habakkuk.

Habakkuk is a prophetic theodicy text; the prophet cries out, questioning God in the midst of suffering and trial while Israel's enemies grow stronger and wealthier. *Whose side is Yahweh on?* "Your eyes [O, God] are too pure to behold evil, and you cannot look on wrongdoing; why do you look on the treacherous and are silent when the wicked swallow those more righteous than they?" (Hab 1:13). The Lord responds with a message for Habakkuk: the justice of God will be manifest at the appointed time, and in the meantime Israel must have faith. This is where the Habakkuk 2:4 slogan comes in. The righteous person must live by faith in God, not by fear and revenge or despair. The simple nature of the phrase "the righteous will live by faith" makes it memorable and easily recitable. But that same simplicity means each of the key words (righteous, live, faith) can be taken in different ways. The word "faith" (Hebrew *emunah*) was often taken in Jewish tradition to refer to fidelity or commitment to the covenant, which is fleshed out in obedience to Torah.[13] Habakkuk 2:4 is also mentioned in an early rabbinic text:

R. Simlai said, "Six hundred and thirteen commandments were given to Moses. . . . Then David came and reduced them to eleven [Ps 15]. Then came Isaiah and reduced them to six [Isa 33:15]. Then came Micah and reduced them to three [Mic 6:8]. Then Isaiah [Isa 56:1]. Then came Amos, and reduced them to one, as it is said, 'Seek me and live' [Amos 5:4]. Or one may then say, then came Habakkuk [2:4] and

---

13. One Qumranic interpretation of Habakkuk takes "live by faith" as careful observation of the Torah commandments and steadfast commitment to their own "Teacher of Righteousness" (see 1QpHab 7.17–8.3).

reduced them to one, as it is said, 'The righteous shall live by his faith/faithfulness.'" (*b.Mak.* 23b)

In this rabbinic text faith/faithfulness associated with Hab 2:4 is understood as commitment to the covenant, which includes the Law's commandments. To live by faith is understood as living with full devotion to the one God and practicing what God has asked of Israel: loyalty, trust, and obedience. When Paul uses Habakkuk 2:4, he does something that was probably unexpected for most Jews—disassociating "faith" (*emunah/pistis*) from the covenantal Law. While Paul's compatriots would have naturally associated Jewish "faith" with living faithfully according to the commandments and laws of Torah, here Paul was separating faith out as a distinct form of religion, i.e., without "works of the Law." This would have been an unprecedented concept from the pen of a first-century Jew, the ancient equivalent of splitting the atom for the first time—*who knew such a thing was even possible?*[14] Paul was in no way throwing out the Old Testament; he wasn't treating the Law as evil or harmful. Rather, he was reorienting the focus of religion, concentrating on a personal relationship with Jesus Christ (i.e., "faith"). Consequently, the Jewish Law must find its place in supporting *that* dynamic, rather than guiding faith in a formal way.

The question has often been raised—*fairly*—"Does Paul quote from Habakkuk faithfully?" From one perspective, we can imagine that Paul was tempted to prooftext Hab 2:4, given its inclusion of the keywords of Paul's gospel: "righteous/just" and "faith" (and even the language of "live";

---

14. Paul was the first New Testament writer to quote Habakkuk 2:4, though this text is also quoted in Hebrews 10:38. The author of Hebrews uses this text to inspire Christian readers toward perseverance in the midst of suffering and persecution. Hebrews compares those who hesitate and shrink back from challenges with those who stay strong in the faith (10:38–39).

Gal 2:20). One can wonder if this verse just jumped out
to Paul as a pithy and convenient motto that comes from
Israel's prophetic tradition and reinforces his message about
the gospel of Jesus Christ. But I think we can say more to
vindicate Paul from the accusation of careless prooftexting;
two observations are worthwhile. First, in early Judaism there
was already an interest in Hab 2:4 as an "essentialization" of
the Jewish religion (as we have seen in the rabbinic text just
cited). Paul was thus giving his take on a "text of interest" for
Jews who were actively discussing the heart of their religion.
Second, while we don't always know whether or to what degree
Paul was inviting readers to look up this Old Testament text
and read the context, if we examine the whole of the book
of Habakkuk it is notable that the focus of this text is on
trust as a personal dynamic and *exclusive worship* as a religious
dynamic. The Law and obedience to Torah's commandments
are not mentioned explicitly. Perhaps keeping the Law is
taken for granted, but the focus of Habakkuk is on a pure
and simple trust in God in the midst of doubt and difficulty.
Habakkuk 2:4 thus serves as a distillation and summary of
the Lord's response to Habakkuk's expression of doubt and
lament: thus the Lord says, "the righteous will live by faith."
Trust me with simple faith, God commands. The people of Israel
are called to stick close to the Lord and put their hope in his
promises to preserve them. To trust others before God is to
trust their gods, and the people must resist the temptation
to make deals with foreign nations just to put their minds
at ease. "The LORD is in his holy temple; let all the earth
keep silence before him!" (Hab 2:20). These final words of
Habakkuk chapter two are an affirmation and reinforcement
of Hab 2:4: *by faith know that the LORD is not idle; trust him no matter what.* That is the essence of faith—a covenantal relationship that goes back to Abraham's simple trust and acceptance

of the voice and presence of God promising a great future of flourishing and thriving. I think it is more than possible that Paul is connecting the dots from Habakkuk back to Genesis and Abraham to demonstrate that the covenant is all about mutuality in faith and trust, and that "works of the Law" must be rethought and reoriented in light of Christ. However, the basic message of the book of Habakkuk has never changed: stay true to God by faith and you will live by God's gracious redemption.

FAITH AS AN ERA: A COVENANTAL APPROACH

If the unlinking of "faith" and "works of the Law" would have been jarring to any Jew reading Galatians, how did Paul explain and defend it in his letter? We can turn to 3:23–29 to follow his argument that this has something to do with eras of God's covenantal history with his people. Paul divides time into two basic eras: the "Law" era and the "faith" era.[15] *Before* the "faith" era, the Law held the people in custody. Paul does not describe this custody as a dungeon with weapons of torture. It is better understood as a period of confinement meant to protect, like a baby being held in a crib. But, just as with the crib, Paul thinks of the Law as restrictive. Once the "faith" era comes, a transition to freedom from the Law follows. I don't think Paul was trying to present the Law as an executor wanting to do harm; still, the "faith" era brings freedom from the Law. If modern readers are confused by these concepts, they can find comfort in knowing that Paul's first readers likely felt similarly. Paul may have anticipated this situation, so he changes gears and uses a different image

---

15. Later Paul mentions a time before the Law period, which we might call the "promise" era (3:17).

than confinement: the household *paidagogos* (literally, "leader of children"):

> Therefore the law was our disciplinarian [*paidagogos*] until
> Christ came, so that we might be justified by faith. (3:24)

As I mentioned in chapter two, this would have been a vivid and insightful metaphor for Paul's readers, but not as helpful for us moderns who don't have such a role in our society. English translations of Galatians have struggled with how to render *paidagogos* in English: "disciplinarian" (NRSV), "guardian" (NET), "tutor" (NASB 1995), and "custodian" (RSV). This male household slave had a few roles, all for the sake of caring for children: taking them to school safely, helping them with their lessons, teaching them a bit of life wisdom, and conducting physical discipline when necessary. We know that some children loved their *paidagogos*, some hated him, and many others had mixed feelings and experiences. Galatians scholars have argued over the years about whether Paul is presenting this *paidagogos* image of the Law in a positive way (tutor, leader) or a negative way (taskmaster, punisher). But in the context of this latter part of Galatians chapter three, the emphasis is on the fact that Greco-Roman household children *grow out of* the need for the *paidagogos*. When children come of age, they become responsible for themselves, whether they had a good *paidagogos* or a bad one. Now, I would suggest that Paul's use of *paidagogos* here is neutral, with perhaps a slant toward the positive—just as this household slave is commissioned by the father to lead the child well, so the Law was given to protect and support Israel. But the *paidagogos*, by nature of his assignment, limits the freedom of the child, and so does the Law for God's people—that's the focus of Paul's argument. The Law, as intended, looked after the people *until*—this "until" is crucial here—Christ came to fulfill the plan that justification (covenantal acceptance and belonging) would come by faith alone (3:24–25).

In Galatians 3:23–25, Paul expresses this fulfillment era of God's covenantal history in two different ways: the coming of *Christ* (3:24) and the coming of *faith* (3:23, 25). The first way is easy to understand: at the fullness of time God sent his Son for the sake of redemption (4:4). But why does Paul use the language of the coming of *faith* (*pistis*)? He cannot be presenting human faith as if it is a brand new concept, because he had begun this chapter by pointing to Abraham as the man of faith in God, a model for believers in Christ. Based on the whole set of arguments Paul makes beginning at 2:15–16 and running through chapter four, he appears to be saying something like this (my paraphrase):

> God began the covenantal journey with Abraham, calling him to faith, a relationship of pure trust: God would make promises and Abraham would walk in God's ways in faith. Then the time of the Law of Moses arrived. The Law did not cancel out Abraham's faith; rather, it provided a structure and system for living by faith, i.e., by keeping the commandments of God. The Law provided boundaries to limit the effects of sin until a permanent solution arrived. God promised his people that there would be a final covenantal dynamic through the Messiah that resembles the intimacy and personal nature of Abraham's relationship with God.

I think the essence of what Paul is saying when he equates the coming of Christ and the coming of "faith" comes down to two things: (1) a deeper and more intimate way of knowing and encountering God (2:20; 4:9); and (2) a covenantal

dynamic of mutuality with God that has been separated
from performance of works of the Law. Christ has opened
up a new pathway for us to become children of God *through
faith* (3:26), justified and made one with Christ and then
able to experience the privileges of full membership in the
Abrahamic family (3:27–29).

FAITH AS FAITHFULNESS

As Paul transitions from the more doctrinal teachings in chapters two through four to the more ethical and applicational
sections of his letter to the Galatians in chapters five and six,
he explicates a great contest of power between the Spirit and
the Flesh. The Flesh seeks to overpower humans through
their sinful desires, and Paul offers examples of the works of
the Flesh like enmities, strife, jealousy, anger, quarrels, dis-
sensions, and factions—in fact, most of the list involves social
evils which frustrate and fracture relationships (5:16–21). On
the other side you have the fruit of the Spirit, which God's
Spirit produces in believers by God's grace: love, joy, peace,
patience, kindness, generosity, faithfulness, gentleness, and
self-control. The majority of this list noticeably involves social
virtues, ways that relationships are strengthened and nurtured.
Love (*agapē*) comes at the beginning, because it is a—if not
the—master virtue of the Christian faith. But also noticeable
is *pistis*, translated by the NRSV as "faithfulness." This would
have been a common social virtue to mention in Jewish and
Greco-Roman traditions—it is all about loyalty and standing
true to your friends and allies. Where the Flesh desires to separate and turn neighbors and partners into enemies, the Spirit
desires to knit together and secure a strong bond of friendship.

This is almost certainly not just general Christian teaching that Paul attaches to this letter. There were real issues of

disagreement and division in Galatia, perhaps over Paul and his gospel. Paul warns his readers in 5:15: "If . . . you bite and devour one another, take care that you are not consumed by one another." Put simply, *antagonism is a recipe for destruction; fights are often ended, but rarely won.* The higher way—the way of Christ and the Spirit—is love and generous service. Paul sums up the whole Law with the commandment "You shall love your neighbor as yourself" (5:14). Wherever Paul has love at the tip of his pen, faith is often on his mind, and vice versa. This is clearly affirmed in Galatians 5:6, where Paul explains that the focus of the Christian life should not be on circumcision (or uncircumcision, for that matter) but "faith working through love."

Given how often Paul uses faith language in Galatians and the slight nuances in various uses, it is sometimes difficult for English translations to know whether to translate *pistis* in any given occurrence as "faith," "faithfulness," "trust," or "allegiance," etc. We know that *pistis* does not mean "works." And yet in 5:6 (just quoted) Paul can talk about *pistis* as "working" (the verbal form of the Greek word "work"; *energeō*). What we do know is that *pistis* in ancient usage tends to mean something more than mental assent, but stops short of action or obedience. Perhaps one way to think about how Paul approaches *pistis* is the English word "devotion." Devotion begins and "lives" (you might say) in the heart and mind, but it is also an active dynamic that attaches to someone or something outside of the self (i.e., devotion to a spouse or children, or devotion to a dream or goal). If "devotion" is a helpful way to think about *pistis*, it is clear from 5:22–23 (the "Fruit of the Spirit") that Paul saw the faith dynamic of Christianity to be true for not only the vertical relationship (devotion to Christ) but also horizontal relationships (devotion to one another).

I see this articulated well in Paul in his commendation of

his friend Philemon: "When I remember you in my prayers,
I always thank my God because I hear of your love for all the
saints and your faith toward the Lord Jesus" (Phlm 4–5). Paul
is appreciating and praising Philemon on both the vertical
and horizontal levels. He uses love (*agapē*) to talk about his
care for the saints (fellow believers) and faith (*pistis*) in relation to Christ, but these run parallel in sentiment and reflect
a Christian's *devotion* to God and all the brothers and sisters.
As I like to tell my students, for Paul faith isn't a "work," but
it *is* always at work.

THE HOUSEHOLD OF FAITH

We see the themes of family and faith come together at the
end of Galatians: "Whenever we have an opportunity, let us
work for the good of all, and especially for those of the family
of faith" (6:10). This is a clear nod to unity in a diverse community. This Galatian community would have been a mix of
Jews and gentiles, slaves and free, and women and men. Their
differences would have been real. There would have been
enduring disagreements about politics, culture, sports, lifestyle, and even religious traditions. But what brought everyone
together was the reality of a new family and household. This
relationship was not of blood, but of faith—a specific faith,
trust, and belonging through Jesus Christ.

FURTHER READING

Bates, Matthew W. *Salvation by Allegiance Alone: Rethinking Faith,
    Works, and the Gospel of Jesus the King.* Grand Rapids: Baker
    Academic, 2017.
Bird, Michael F., and Preston M. Sprinkle, eds. *The Faith of Jesus
    Christ: Exegetical, Biblical, and Theological Studies.* Peabody, MA:
    Hendrickson, 2009.

Gorman, Michael J. *Becoming the Gospel: Paul, Participation, and Mission.* Grand Rapids: Eerdmans, 2015.

Gupta, Nijay K. *Paul and the Language of Faith.* Grand Rapids: Eerdmans, 2020.

Morgan, Teresa. *The New Testament and The Theology of Trust: "This Rich Trust."* Oxford: Oxford University Press, 2022.

———. *Roman Faith and Christian Faith:* Pistis *and* Fides *in the Early Roman Empire and Early Churches.* Oxford: Oxford University Press, 2015.

CHAPTER 5

Freedom: Divine Empowerment to Choose Service and Love

Especially since the Reformation era, Protestants have often associated Galatians with the theological theme of freedom. In the modern era we can look to Merrill Tenney (*Galatians: The Charter of Christian Liberty*), Leon Morris (*Galatians: Paul's Charter of Christian Freedom*), and Richard N. Longenecker (*Paul, Apostle of Liberty*, heavily influenced by Galatians).[1] Martin Luther's Commentary on Galatians makes much of Paul's discussion of freedom, especially in 5:1. Luther talks about this verse outlining Paul's "doctrine of Christian liberty," which contrasts "everlasting liberty" with "everlasting slavery."[2] The former, Luther argues, is found in Christ; the latter is tied to the Law. We will come back to the

---

1. Merrill Tenney, *Galatians: The Charter of Christian Liberty* (Grand Rapids: Eerdmans, 1957); Richard N. Longenecker, *Paul, Apostle of Liberty*, 2nd ed. (Grand Rapids: Eerdmans, 2015); Leon Morris, *Galatians: Paul's Charter of Christian Freedom* (Downers Grove: InterVarsity Press, 1996); see also Quentin Quesnell, *The Gospel of Christian Freedom* (New York: Herder & Herder, 1969) and C. K. Barrett, *Freedom and Obligation: A Study of the Epistle to the Galatians* (Philadelphia: Westminster Press, 1985).

2. See Martin Luther, *Martin Luther's Commentary on Saint Paul's Epistle to the Galatians (1535): Lecture Notes Transcribed by Students & Presented in Today's English*, trans. Haroldo Camacho (Irvine, CA: 1517 Publishing, 2018).

Law later in this chapter. For now, I simply want to point out that many interpreters of Galatians throughout the years have noticed that in this letter Paul dwells on the subject of *freedom* and its natural opposite, *slavery*. To some it might seem obvious that freedom's counterpart is slavery. Yet this is worth emphasizing, because in non-slave societies (like twenty-first century America) "freedom" is often discussed as a political value, but its opposite is viewed as things like restriction of rights, persecution, subjugation, or simply busyness ("are you 'free' this afternoon?"). Freedom, in modern discourse, is about the lack of constraints or limitations—"you are 'free' to move about the cabin"—and therefore there are endless applications.[3] However, in ancient usage the Greek word *eleutheria* ("freedom") is a technical term and was normally understood as a binary (free vs. slave; Gal 3:28). Used metaphorically (as Paul does), freedom could be applied to many different things, but the point worth making here is that conceptually freedom had primarily one opposite: slavery. Paul talks about theological slavery many times throughout his letters, but in fact he rarely discusses freedom. Thus, the theme of freedom is distinctive in Galatians as Paul urges these believers to embrace freedom and not willingly shackle themselves (back) into slavery. Here is a brief overview of how freedom language is used by Paul in this letter:

> But because of false believers secretly brought in, who slipped in to spy on the freedom we have in Christ Jesus, so that they might enslave us—we did not submit to them even for a moment, so that the truth of the gospel might always remain with you. (2:4–5)

---

3. See Richard Bauckham, *God and the Crisis of Freedom: Biblical and Contemporary Perspectives* (Louisville: Westminster John Knox Press, 2002): "Freedom has all the power and all the danger of a radically under-determined notion," 2.

In this early part of the letter, Paul recounts a special Jerusalem meeting where he presented his gospel message to the apostolic leadership to join forces on behalf of the gentile mission to which he was called by Jesus Christ himself. We know the ultimate success of this meeting from Paul's perspective: the apostles extended to Paul (and Barnabas) the "right hand of fellowship" (2:9). But there was also opposition; Paul mentions certain "false brothers" who didn't like his dangerous message of freedom, presumably in relation to Paul not requiring circumcision for gentiles. Thankfully, Paul did not back down: he remained faithful to the "truth of the gospel" and rejected any attempt to obligate the gentiles toward circumcision or any other form of mandatory Law observance.

In chapter four, Paul vividly reads the stories of Abraham and his progeny in terms of a freedom–slavery dichotomy:

Tell me, you who desire to be subject to the law, will you not listen to the law? For it is written that Abraham had two sons, one by a slave woman and the other by a free woman. One, the child of the slave, was born according to the flesh; the other, the child of the free woman, was born through the promise. Now this is an allegory: these women are two covenants. One woman, in fact, is Hagar, from Mount Sinai, bearing children for slavery. Now Hagar is Mount Sinai in Arabia and corresponds to the present Jerusalem, for she is in slavery with her children. But the other woman corresponds to the Jerusalem above; she is free, and she is our mother. For it is written,

"Rejoice, you childless one, you who bear no children,
     burst into song and shout, you who endure no
                   birth pangs;

> for the children of the desolate woman are more
>   numerous
>   than the children of the one who is married."
>
> Now you, my friends, are children of the promise, like Isaac. But just as at that time the child who was born according to the flesh persecuted the child who was born according to the Spirit, so it is now also. But what does the scripture say? "Drive out the slave and her child; for the child of the slave will not share the inheritance with the child of the free woman." So then, friends, we are children, not of the slave but of the free woman. (4:21–31)

This passage is fraught with interpretive mysteries and landmines. (*Is this an allegory? Is it the only way to read these stories? Does Hagar represent "Judaism," "Jewish Christianity," or some false and distorted form of Christianity propagated by false teachers?*) We don't have space to address these questions.[4] What we can say here is that Paul calls the Galatian Christians (most of whom are gentiles) to consider two paths, the line of Hagar and the line of Sarah (who is not named, though Isaac is). Paul begins with the notion that one is a slave line (Hagar) and one is a free line (Sarah) (4:22). The former is flesh; the latter is divine promise. They represent two opposing covenants: one is destined for eternal slavery, the other for freedom in the heavenly Jerusalem. What is required of the Galatians is that they heed the call of Genesis 21:10: "Cast out this slave woman with her son." As Paul interprets it, this means the Galatians must have nothing to do with a covenant that comes from slavery and has no hope of freedom. I have talked about Paul's view of the Law elsewhere

---

4. See my commentary notes, *Galatians*, SGBC, 194–205.

in this book (see especially the introduction); it is sufficient to say here that although Paul is associating an obligation of circumcision with slavery, this does not mean he viewed the Law as contrary to the gospel (3:21). Paul was not criticizing the Mosaic covenant here, which guided Israel for hundreds of years and is naturally associated with Isaac (not Ishmael).

> For freedom Christ has set us free. Stand firm, therefore, and do not submit again to a yoke of slavery. (5:1)

Paul's letter comes to a climax with 5:1, bridging the "two covenants" teaching of 4:21–31 and the following section beginning with the more direct exhortation in 5:2 (*Ide!*, "Listen!" or "Pay attention!"). The choices that lie before the Galatians, from Paul's vantage point, are slavery and freedom. The Galatians themselves didn't see it that way, but Paul did. The matter is reinforced in 5:13a: "For you were called to freedom." While Paul occasionally mentions freedom in other letters (2 Cor 3:17), it is a dominant theme in Galatians.

ISRAEL'S JOURNEY TO FREEDOM

Israel had clung to the promise and dream of "freedom" since the days of Moses. The book of Exodus (from the Greek word *exodos*, "the way out of [slavery]") narrates the liberation of Israel, a contest of power between Yahweh and Egypt's pharaoh. Yahweh claims the people of Israel as his own and leads them to the special land he has marked out for them, so they can be a holy nation and priestly kingdom. The rest of the Old Testament tells a difficult tale of ups and downs in Israel's national life, with almost endless wars and feuds with the Canaanites and a devastating siege at the hands of Assyria.

Israel was forced out of its land into exile in Babylon, then handed over to Persian rule. While the people were allowed to return to their homeland to settle again and rebuild their temple, they rarely enjoyed political "freedom." In the middle of the second century BCE, the famous Maccabean revolt took place against a Greco-Syrian tyrant called Antiochus IV ("Epiphanes"). We find the language of freedom associated with these pious Jews' commitment to preserving not only their national independence, but defending their religion and covenantal life (1 Macc 14:26).

In the New Testament, you can sense some political sensitivities in the Jewish community when Jesus promises truth that will lead to freedom through his message of eternal life. Some of his hearers respond, "We are descendants of Abraham and have never been slaves to anyone. What do you mean by saying, 'You will be made free?'" (John 8:33). Obviously, these Jews were not fully understanding Jesus's message, which was not just about the restoration of an earthly nation. Jesus had a similar conversation with his apostles at the beginning of the book of Acts. They asked him, "Lord, is this the time when you will restore the kingdom to Israel?" (Acts 1:6). Jesus didn't answer their question with a simple "yes" or "no," but indicated his thinking about the kingdom by pointing to the bestowal of the Holy Spirit and the worldwide mission of the gospel. It is true that the language of "restoration," which is parallel to the concept of freedom, is used throughout the Old Testament and is especially prominent in the Prophets, who foretold national freedom and covenantal flourishing (Jer 24:6; 27:19–22; Ezek 17:23; cf. 1 Macc 15:3; 2 Macc 11:25). But the gospel of Jesus the Messiah involves not just good news for one nation, Israel, but prosperity, freedom, and flourishing for the whole world *through* Israel and Israel's Messiah.

THE SLAVERY/FREEDOM PARADOX

Returning to Paul again, it is helpful to process his conception of freedom by looking at his theological use of slavery
language. First of all, Paul more commonly uses slavery imagery in his letters than freedom imagery, though they belong
together conceptually. Secondly, contrary to what one might
expect, Paul does not conceive of slavery and freedom as
exclusive opposites; we don't see statements like *freedom is the
absence of slavery* or *slavery is the absence of freedom*. A number
of times, Paul actually represents the gospel and faith in
Jesus Christ *as* slavery (all translations adapted to emphasize
the term):

> . . . you turned to God from idols, to serve [as a slave][5] the
> living and true God. (1 Thess 1:9)

> Paul, a slave of Jesus Christ. (Rom 1:1; cf. Titus 1.1)

> Serve the Lord *as a slave*. (Rom 12:11)[6]

> The one who serves[7] Christ *as a slave to a master* is acceptable
> to God. (Rom 14:18a)

> [Of troublemakers in the church:] Such people do not
> serve[8] our Lord Christ *as a slave to a master* but their own
> appetites. (Rom 16:18a)

---

5. The verb Paul uses here (*douleuō*) comes from the noun *doulos*, which
means "slave." Worship of the one God is described as the kind of "service" a slave
gives to a master.

6. Again, the verb here is *douleuō*.

7. *douleuō*.

8. *douleuō*.

If I were still pleasing people, I would not be a slave of Christ. (Gal 1:10)

Paul and Timothy, slaves of Christ Jesus. (Phil 1:1)

You serve[9] the Lord Christ *as a slave to a master.* (Col 3:24)

To be a Christian, in Paul's mind, is to be a devoted slave of Christ. Thus, Paul prefers to call Jesus "Lord" (*kyrios*, which is the same term for a slave's "master").[10] Perhaps he was influenced by Jesus's own teaching in Matt 6:24: "No one can serve two masters, for a slave will either hate the one and love the other or be devoted to the one and despise the other. You cannot serve God and *mammon.*"[11] Jesus and the apostles argue that the one God deserves *exclusive* and *complete* devotion, and the social dynamic of slavery was well-suited to express this point.[12] Slaves were not in control of their own lives; they had no agency in regard to their present or future. They lived to honor, please, and carry out the will of their master.

At the same time, Paul can also express that the gospel is all about *freedom.* The one God is a *liberating* God. The gospel, by nature, is an *invitation: Come! Believe! Be baptized!* There is choice, there is agency, there is freedom. Sometimes this is a matter of perspective. For instance, Paul explains to the Corinthians: "For whoever was called in the Lord as a slave is a freed person belonging to the Lord, just as whoever was

---

9. *douleuō.*

10. This language and imagery is also found in other apostolic writings, such as James 1:1; 2 Peter 1:1; Jude 1; Rev 1:1.

11. *Mammon* is an Aramaic word referring to material wealth. See, similarly, 2 Peter 2:19.

12. Murray J. Harris, *Slave of Christ: A New Testament Metaphor for Total Devotion to Christ* (Downers Grove: IVP Academic, 2001).

free when called is a slave of Christ" (1 Cor 7:22). In fact, these two theological affirmations are true for both slaves and free persons: freedom in Christ and slavery to Christ are not exclusive opposites, or only sometimes or partially true; they are two sides of the same gospel coin.

The truth of the matter is, there is no pure or absolute freedom in this world. Everyone has a boss. Or commitments. Or compulsions. Age can control mortals—or health, or money, or fear. For Paul, the good news of Jesus is not about becoming free to do *whatever* one wants (good or evil), but to be freed from sin to become what one was meant to be: to flourish under the *right* master. Paul offers an extensive teaching to the Romans along these lines. In Romans 6, he explains that believers who have been buried with Christ in baptism are dead to the old masters called Sin and Death and raised to a new life (6:3–7). The chains of bondage to Sin are broken (6:6). However, this freedom from Sin is not unto pure autonomy, because you might find yourself quickly smuggled into another form of bondage by a different master. Rather, believers immediately transition from slaves to Sin to slaves to Christ and his priority of righteousness (6:18). It is a bit like young athletes suffering under an abusive team coach. Let's say that coach is fired—*good riddance!* But the team benefits very little *as a team* by no longer having a coach at all. A team needs a coach, but what it really needs is a *good* coach—someone who will help its members flourish. A good coach gives players agency (trusts them to make judgments in the moment), but also presses them to be fully committed to their teammates and avoid drawing needless attention to themselves at the cost of other teammates (i.e., showboating). Paul expresses a similar notion in 1 Corinthians 9:19: "For though I am free with respect to all, I have made myself a slave to all, so that I might win more of them."

Across the New Testament, various writers address the dangers of "pure" freedom—the idea that it is healthy and good to be able to do *whatever* you want. Paul deliberately reiterates to the Corinthians that Christian "freedom" is not a license to act on selfish whims and wishes. For instance, one might say, "all things are permitted," but the qualifier "not all things are beneficial" must be added (1 Cor 10:23 NRSVue). It is all too easy to wave around a banner of "freedom" and use it as an excuse to harm other people. Paul warns the Galatians: "You were called to freedom, brothers and sisters; only do not use your freedom as an opportunity for self-indulgence; but through love become slaves to one another" (5:13). Thus, life-giving "freedom" is the ability to choose and commit oneself to doing good to others. This is also well-expressed in 1 Peter: "As [slaves] of God, live as free people, yet do not use your freedom as a pretext for evil" (1 Peter 2:16).

TRUE FREEDOM IN GRECO-ROMAN PHILOSOPHICAL DISCOURSE

We have just noted that "freedom" can be understood from different perspectives. A more literal and technical use of freedom language relates on the personal level to manumission from slavery.[13] On a national level, "freedom" pertains to liberation from colonial occupation and control. We also find philosophers, especially during the classical era of Greek history, reflecting on the existential nature of freedom. For example, Aristotle, the famous philosopher, addresses different attitudes toward freedom and how it can be misconceived and abused. In his discussion of the interplay between

---

13. "Manumission" is the technical term for granting a slave's legal freedom.

personal freedom and the rule of government leaders, he differentiates between justice, equality, and freedom. Aristotle argues that if the multitude of the populace gets to decide what is legal and "freedom" is conceived of as "doing whatever one wants," then anarchy and chaos will follow.[14] He quotes Euripides's definition of freedom as doing whatever one finds pleasing.[15] This can be conceived of as fighting against laws and rules, because these can be perceived as restricting this sort of "freedom." But, Aristotle explains, "to live in conformity with the constitution ought not to be considered slavery, but safety."[16] Aristotle is one of the early formative Greek thinkers on "freedom" who goes above and beyond the categories of legal freedom from slavery or conquest. These philosophers were using "freedom" language to talk about human flourishing; this later became articulated in American political discourse as "life, liberty, and the pursuit of happiness" (from the Declaration of Independence).

As these conversations developed in the Greco-Roman world, it became more common for philosophers to associate "true freedom" with a state of mind. This was especially popular among Stoic thinkers. The Greek philosopher Epictetus (c. CE 50–c. CE 135), for instance, was a manumitted slave. I assume he valued his legal freedom, yet he regularly talked about the importance of living with a certain liberation mindset. Stoics were known for living with an acceptance of fate and seeking contentment in the midst of difficult circumstances. Epictetus writes,

---

14. "*to ho ti an boulētai tis poiein*," Arist. *Pol.* 5.9.1310a.

15. We cannot find this exact quote in Euripides's extant literature.

16. The Greek word Aristotle uses here that is translated "safety" is *sōteria* (commonly translated "salvation" in the Greek New Testament). See the helpful discussion in F. Stanley Jones, "Freedom," in *The Anchor Yale Bible Dictionary*, ed. David Noel Freedman (New York: Doubleday, 1992), 856.

Our master is anyone who has the power to implement or prevent the things that we want or don't want. Whoever wants to be free, therefore, should wish for nothing or avoid nothing that is up to other people. Failing that, one is bound to be a slave. (*Enchiron.* 14; cf. 1 *Discourses* 12.8)

Epictetus uses the emotional states as a diagnostic of whether one is truly free. Those who are constantly driven to extremes—fear, sorrow, anger, anxiety—prove that they are slaves to their circumstances. Education in the way of the Stoics, he believed, is the only path to freedom and peace (*2 Disc.* 1.22–25). Similar arguments about freedom are made by the Roman Stoic Seneca (4 BCE to CE 65). In his letter to Lucilius (Letter 47), Seneca talks about the phenomenon of slavery in Roman society. While Seneca does not argue for the end of the institution of slavery, he makes the case that masters should be civil toward their slaves and not treat them as lesser people, because all people are slaves in some way or another. If masters show patience and generosity toward slaves, then Fortune may be kind to these compassionate masters (47.11–12). Seneca imagined that people will argue that they have freedom and are under no obligation to anyone. He countered that "masters" come in all forms: someone might be "a slave to lust, another to greed, another to ambition, and all men are slaves to fear. I will name you an ex-consul who is a slave to an old hag, a millionaire who is a slave to a serving-maid; I will show you youths of the noblest birth in serfdom to pantomime players! No servitude is more disgraceful than that which is self-imposed!" (47.17).

Within the stream of these kinds of Greco-Roman conversations, we find a number of Jewish writers talking about liberation from a moral philosophical perspective of lifestyle and attitude. For example, the author of *4 Maccabees* hails "reason" (*logismoi*) as more royal than kings and freer than the free (*4 Macc.* 14.2). But the most extensive philosophical discussion of freedom is found in the work of the Jewish philosopher Philo of Alexandria, especially in his tractate called *Every Good Man Is Free*.[17] Along the same lines as Epictetus and Seneca, Philo argues that the free are not always truly free, and legal slaves are not always really in bondage. There are, he explains, two kinds of slavery: one of the body and another of the soul. It is all too easy for the vice of wickedness or desire to take control of the soul and lead to a darker slavery than the legal kind (17). What can free people from this soul bondage? They must submit to God and commit themselves to virtue:

> But then a man is happy, inasmuch as he bears within himself the foundation and complement of virtue and excellence, in which consists the supreme power over all things . . . so that beyond all controversy and of necessity the virtuous man is free. (41; cf. 61)

So, Philo warns his readers that it is not enough for a slave to seek worldly manumission. All men are easily dominated by their own desires and appetites (Philo happens to mention addiction to cheesecake, of all things!) (*Free* 156; cf. 503). It is more than possible that Philo's philosophical reflections on freedom drew inspiration from Cicero's fifth claim in his *Stoic Paradoxes*: "The Wise Man Alone Is Free, and Every Fool Is a Slave." Cicero defined "freedom" as acting on the basis of choice, not compulsion. Yes, slave masters compel,

---

17. Philo wrote another work, now lost, called *Every Bad Man Is a Slave*; see Maren R. Niehoff, *Philo of Alexandria: An Intellectual Biography* (New Haven: Yale University Press, 2018), 81.

but so do internal desires and infatuations, whether lust or greed. Freedom can only come from holding loosely to possessions, women, and status, Cicero urged, so that one can truly embrace the best option in any given circumstance: the *virtuous* path (Stoic Paradoxes 5.34).

GALATIANS 2: FREEDOM AND THE LAW

As we turn again to Galatians, we see that Paul was also engaging in the broader philosophical conversation about "inner" freedom. He preferred to frame this in terms of resisting the Flesh (*sarks*) and embracing the transformative work of God's Spirit. We will address Paul's theological understanding of Flesh and Spirit soon. First, it is important to explain how the language of freedom relates to Paul's concerns about the Jewish Law, since that is one of the main concerns of Galatians. As I described earlier, Galatians was written because false teachers were encouraging the (mostly gentile) Galatians to commit themselves to the Jewish Law by undergoing the ritual of circumcision, in order to be justified before God and become *bona fide* members of the Abrahamic family. By the time Paul wrote this letter, the Galatians were on the verge of agreeing to these terms (5:2–3).

Paul, consequently, reminds the Galatians that he preached freedom to them when they first embraced the gospel: freedom from fear, freedom from the flesh, and freedom to love one another. If they made this commitment to the Jewish Law through circumcision, it would be a step backward in their faith, not a step forward: "For freedom Christ has set us free. Stand firm, therefore, and do not submit again to a yoke of slavery" (5:1).

Paul was opposing a Christian faction that wanted to require Law obedience for gentiles. This was no small matter; in fact, it was a matter of justification and salvation. In Galatians, this topic comes up for the first time when Paul mentions the Jerusalem summit where he and Barnabas presented their ministry to the Judean Christian leadership. There Paul encountered certain opponents, whom he refers to as interlopers "spying" on the "freedom" believers had in Christ Jesus, ultimately wanting to trade this liberty for slavery (2:4). Given that circumcision was the topic of conversation (with Titus present as a model of the uncircumcised gentile Christian), Paul was contrasting a gospel of freedom (no Law requirement) with a gospel of slavery (Law requirement). From other writings of Paul, we know that he had no concern with Jews or gentiles choosing to observe certain Jewish traditions or practices as a preference (e.g., Rom 14:5–6). But *requiring* circumcision and Law obedience was different; this deviated from the *truth of the gospel*. Paul drew a line in the sand in his letter to the Galatians, and he forced them to make a decision for freedom or for slavery. Their agreement to circumcision would reveal their choice:

> Listen! I, Paul, am telling you that if you let yourselves be circumcised, Christ will be of no benefit to you. Once again I testify to every man who lets himself be circumcised that he is obligated to obey the entire law. You who want to be justified by the law have cut yourselves off from Christ; you have fallen away from grace. (5:2–4)

These are strong words—do-or-die words—but notice what Paul does *not* say. He does not say that Jews ought to be ashamed of their circumcision. Later in Galatians 5–6 he repeats that uncircumcision is no better than circumcision; what matters is how one sees the act (5:6; 6:15; cf. 1 Cor 7:19). Paul does not say that the Galatians will be cursed for reading the Law or for gaining wisdom from it; in fact, Paul himself quoted the Law approvingly (5:14). But in *this* moment, if the Galatians agreed to circumcision they would be questioning the sufficiency of Christ for justification. They would be treating circumcision as a kind of secondary mechanism for entering the family of God. For Paul, that line of thinking was *disastrous*. This would be tantamount to seeking to be "justified by the Law" (5:4), and grasping the Law for this purpose would mean letting go of Christ. In other words, if the Galatians bound themselves to the Law in this way, they would be giving up the *freedom* in Christ they had first sought to embrace. What exactly is Paul's concern with the Law? Why do believers need to be free from the Law, if God himself gave the Law as a good gift to Israel (Rom 9:4)? We will look at Paul's conception of the Law in terms of two frames he uses in Galatians: the Law as *confinement* and the Law as *paidagogos*.

Law as Confinement

Starting in 3:21a, Paul raises the question that was probably on the minds of many Galatian believers—is the Law opposed to the (Abrahamic) promises of God? Paul's answer is that these are not in tension, because the Law was never intended to be a salvation mechanism for the people of God. While the Law could diagnose wrongdoing, it never had the capacity to bring about righteousness (3:21b). Paul's words in 3:22 are meant to offer further explanation of the purpose and function of the Law, but have been interpreted in various ways by scholars:

> But the scripture has *imprisoned* all things under the power of sin, so that what was promised through faith in Jesus Christ might be given to those who believe. (NRSV)

But the Scripture has *confined* everyone under sin, so that
the promise by faith in Jesus Christ might be given to those
who believe. (NASB)

But Scripture has *locked up* everything under the control of
sin, so that what was promised, being given through faith
in Jesus Christ, might be given to those who believe. (NIV)

The Greek word represented in the italics is *synkleiō*, and
can be translated and interpreted variously based on context. The most basic meaning of *synkleiō* is "to confine" or
"to enclose." The NRSV's choice to interpret this as "impris-
oned" takes *synkleiō* in a negative sense of the Law's hostility
toward humans. The NIV appears to adopt a similar reading ("locked up"). But the NASB's more neutral approach
makes it unclear whether the Law was protecting or harming
humans. Paul addresses the matter again in the next verse by
using *synkleiō* again as well as another verb, *phroureō*, which
means "to guard" (3:23). That verb tends to be used in a positive way: for keeping someone or something safe from harm
(Phil 4:7; 1 Pet 1:5). What Paul appears to be saying is that the
Law played a role of holding the people of God in custody
(presumably for their own protection) until such a time as
they could be made righteous by Jesus Christ through faith.

The combination of the verbs *synkleiō* ("to confine") and
phroureō ("to guard") are probably meant to express some
ambivalence about the function of the Law. On the positive
side, the Law provided boundaries and barriers that shielded
Israel from negative outside influences. However, because it
could not solve the problem of sin, but only limit it, the Law
could become a snare if Israel used it wrongly, treating it as
the means of salvation. When I am teaching on Paul's view
of the Law in Christ, I like to use the analogy of a baby crib.

When babies are small, the crib is used to protect them and keep them from harming themselves. It restricts their movement and keeps them near the parent. However, as children get older, the crib loses its function and value, and can even become a hazard. If children try to climb out of it (and succeed), they could hurt themselves. If children become too attached to the crib and don't want to switch to a bed, the crib could stunt their development. All along, the goal of growing up is to leave the crib, even though the crib is good and necessary for a specific period of development. In the same way, from Paul's perspective, the Law had an important role of confining Israel in a certain era, but only *until* the time of Christ and a new era of faith (see chapter three in this book). When the Law is used for the wrong purposes in the wrong stage, it becomes a hazard. Just as never leaving a crib inhibits the freedom that older children need in order to flourish, so too the people of God cannot grow properly in their faith if they stay confined under the Law. This brings us to the second key image Paul uses regarding the problem of the Law: its limited role of *paidagogos*.

Law as Paidagogos

We have already talked about Paul's metaphor of the *paidagogos* (pp. 12, 45–46): the male slave in a Greco-Roman household taking charge of a free child of the house and acting as a combination of life tutor, bodyguard, and disciplinarian. Paul compares the Law to this role for Israel, but he was not intending to imply that a *paidagogos* was inherently virtuous (like a guardian angel) or evil (like a cruel nanny). Rather, the *temporary* nature of the *paidagogos* is the focus: "Therefore the law was our *paidagogos* until Christ came, so that we might be justified by faith" (3:24). While not everyone had a *paidagogos* (not all households wanted or could afford slaves), this slave was a stock character in many literary and theatrical stories. And, therefore, virtually every reader of Galatians would have known that household children grow out of their need for a *paidagogos*.

Also, in chapter four Paul makes an important additional point about Greco-Roman family life. Children have a tenuous status in the household before they reach adulthood (4:1–2). They are not yet fully family; that is, they are not heirs of the household but only *potential* heirs. Paul says that children have the same status as slaves, which is a bit of an exaggeration, but he is making the point that children are meant to grow up. Staying a minor forever, if it were possible, in effect means that children can never truly embrace being a part of the family. As they mature and reach adulthood, they naturally say goodbye to the *paidagogos* and embrace the responsibilities of being a contributing part of the family, which involves both new responsibilities and new freedoms.

Paul's purpose in using this image of the *paidagogos* is to reinforce his point that the Law's role is not eternal and central, but temporary and preparatory. The Law was always meant to play the part of a companion and aid until a new era arrived where it was not needed. Clinging to the Law in the era of faith and fulfillment would stunt the church's growth and prohibit believers from fully embracing Christ.

What does "freedom" from the Law look like for Paul? It does not look like dismissal of the Law, and certainly not antagonism. Paul did not view the Law as a burden that cannot be carried, nor was it a tormentor. In order to put Paul's freedom language into context (of the Galatian situation), we have to see that he was reacting *against* the rival teachers' attempts to compel the Galatians through fear to keep the commandments of the Law and adopt circumcision. The Galatians were fearful that they would not otherwise find justification before God, nor would they be worthy to become a part of God's great family.

GALATIANS: FREEDOM AND THE FLESH

The subject of how Paul uses the language of "flesh" (*sarks*) is complex, and it is not possible to give a full discussion here.[18] It suffices to say that we can delineate at least three different ways Paul uses "flesh". First, you have the neutral meaning: "flesh" as in skin, bones, and blood (1:16). This is a reference to human beings in their materiality and mortality. When Paul refers to life "in the flesh," sometimes he simply means day-to-day human life (2:20b). Secondly, Paul uses "flesh" to indicate a primal state of being where we act according to self-serving desires (1 Cor 3:3; Gal 3:3; 6:8). The third use of "flesh" language is a bit difficult to detect and explain; it appears that Paul sometimes uses "flesh" (*sarks*) to talk about an entity that can dominate human beings, like an evil power or force. We see this most clearly in Galatians 5:16–17: "Live by the Spirit, I say, and do not gratify the desires of the flesh. For what the flesh desires is opposed to the Spirit, and what the Spirit desires is opposed to the flesh; for these are opposed to each other, to prevent you from doing what you want." Spirit and Flesh are presented as primordial enemies, horns locked in an eternal battle for the souls of mortals. However, it is difficult to discern when Paul is talking about our personal inner desires and temptations or this power called "Flesh"—this is because they are often intertwined.[19]

---

18. See Timothy Gombis, "Flesh," in *Dictionary of Paul and His Letters: A Compendium of Contemporary Biblical Scholarship*, ed. Scot McKnight, Lynn Cohick, and Nijay K. Gupta, 2nd ed. (Downers Grove: IVP Academic, 2023), 314–19.

19. See Beverly Roberts Gaventa, *When in Romans: An Invitation to Linger with the Gospel according to Paul* (Grand Rapids: Baker Academic, 2018), 23–46.

While we cannot always know for certain exactly which use of *sarks* Paul intended, it is clear that he proclaimed freedom from the domination of these negative desires and forces. Now, "freedom" doesn't mean those desires simply evaporate! Paul would have had a lot more free time on his hands if that were the case. While the "chains" of bondage may be broken by the work of Christ and the Spirit, old habits die hard. Paul explains to the Galatians: "You were called to freedom, brothers and sisters; only do not use your freedom as an opportunity for self-indulgence [*sarks*]" (5:13a). Here it is apparent that Paul is engaging in that wider philosophical discourse about freedom and the morality of choice we discussed earlier: choosing what is good and righteous rather than giving in to temptation and choosing what is self-serving. Paul goes on to point to the two paths: the way of the Flesh and the way of the Spirit. The Flesh's works fall into two categories: twisted desires and social evils. In the first type we have sexual impurity, idolatry, and drunkenness (etc.). In the second type we have jealousy, anger, and strife (etc.). Both of these types are self-serving and do ultimate harm to self and/or the other. Paul's proclamation of freedom from the Flesh means the choice now belongs with believers to either give in to the Flesh or to resist the Flesh and walk in step with the Spirit. The fruit of the Spirit is well-known in Christian tradition: love, joy, peace, patience, kindness, generosity, faithfulness, gentleness, and self-control (5:22–23). These are the opposite of the Flesh. The Flesh craves disunity, hatred, and unrestrained desires taking control, but the Spirit cultivates self-control and communal flourishing through care and concern for the other. For Christians, the dominating power of the Flesh has been taken away since "those who belong to Christ Jesus have crucified the flesh [*sarks*] with its passions and desires" (5:24). Christ has enabled free choice for believers; they are no longer dominated and mastered by the desires of the *sarks*. They can choose—but it takes maturity, humility, and wisdom to choose what the Spirit wants. Later on Paul calls this sowing to the Spirit rather than sowing to the Flesh (6:8).

FREEDOM TO LOVE

Paul is clear in Galatians that the "freedom" found in the gospel is about being untethered from any kind of master, whether Law or death or the Flesh. The gospel brings empowerment and liberation to allow the believer in Jesus to *choose*— but choose what? Many Greco-Roman philosophers would say "choose the good." Or "choose to be at peace with fate." Paul would have been in some alignment with these ideas, but he had a specific keyword in mind for the orientation of one's freedom: love (*agapē*). As we have already noted, Paul exhorts the Galatians that they need to choose freedom rather than go back to slavery, but gospel freedom is not an excuse for choosing to give in to the Flesh (*sarks*; 5:13a). Rather, this freedom is an opportunity to choose to serve one another. Paul can talk about slavery in different ways, sometimes as a burden relieved by liberation (5:1) but at other times as a personal decision motivated by love: "Through love become slaves to one another" (5:13b). Paul's focus here is not on enslavement per se, but on deep care and concern for the other. He sums up the whole of the Law by quoting Leviticus 19:18: "You shall love your neighbor as yourself" (Gal 5:14).[20] Christian freedom means cutting the bonds of devotion to

---

20. This is quoted numerous times throughout the New Testament (Matt 5:43; 19:19; 22:39; Mark 12:31; Rom 13:9; James 2:8). For a thorough study of this verse in early Judaism, see Kengo Akiyama, *The Love of Neighbour in Ancient Judaism*, AJEC 105 (Boston: Brill, 2018).

the Law or addiction to satisfying the carnal desires, and dedicating oneself to caring for others. Love is so important to Paul that it could be a key theme of Galatians by itself. Love begins, for Paul, with Christ "who loved me and gave himself for me" (2:20; cf. Rom 8:32). Love involves affection, but its ultimate expression is self-donation, culminating in the case of Christ's death. This love is even more unique because Christ died for *sinners*:

> For while we were still weak, at the right time Christ died for the ungodly. Indeed, rarely will anyone die for a righteous person—though perhaps for a good person someone might actually dare to die. But God proves his love for us in that while we still were sinners Christ died for us. Much more surely then, now that we have been justified by his blood, will we be saved through him from the wrath of God. For if while we were enemies, we were reconciled to God through the death of his Son, much more surely, having been reconciled, will we be saved by his life. But more than that, we even boast in God through our Lord Jesus Christ, through whom we have now received reconciliation. (Rom 5:6–11)

This example in the story of Christ becomes the inspiration for Christian love. Believers are freed from sin and Flesh thanks to the loving actions of Christ, and through the Spirit this freedom affords them the ability to serve and show devotion to one another, imitating God's love in Jesus Christ. Faith is not true or genuine unless it converts into love (5:6). This probably indicates that Paul intentionally placed *agapē* at the beginning of his list of the fruit of the Spirit. Love is the master virtue that drives all the others (5:22–23). Fear and bondage restrict the will, but freedom opens people up to living out their true vocation in conformity with the Son of God: to love genuinely, freely, and deeply.

SUGGESTED READING

Bauckham, Richard. *God and the Crisis of Freedom: Biblical and Contemporary Perspectives*. Louisville: Westminster John Knox Press, 2002.

Campbell, Douglas A. *Pauline Dogmatics: The Triumph of God's Love*. Grand Rapids: Eerdmans, 2020.

Longenecker, Richard N. *Paul, Apostle of Liberty*. 2nd ed. Grand Rapids: Eerdmans, 2015.

Justification in Galatians

In this book we have focused on the themes of family, faith, and freedom in Galatians. Because Paul's language of justification has been a matter of vigorous debate over the centuries, and continues to be a hot topic in recent discussions of Paul's theology, I thought it would be beneficial to discuss the background and state of this debate even though I don't treat justification as one of the core "themes."

JUSTIFICATION LANGUAGE

Before looking closely at Paul's use of justification language, it's important to understand the Greek terms involved and how they are translated in traditional English Bibles. The key words are part of the Greek *dikaios* family:

Dikaios. This Greek word means "just" or "right." It relates to behavior in accord with a certain standard. For example, the Septuagint text of Proverbs claims that honest measurement scales of a merchant are *dikaios* before the Lord (Prov 11:1). They are honest, good, and meet God's standard of proper conduct.

Dikaiosyne. *Dikaios* is an adjective ("right"); *dikaiosyne* is a noun form. When *dikaiosyne* is used in reference to a moral attribute it is translated in English Bibles as "righteousness," although it is not an inherently religious term. It simply refers to "right-ness," and can also refer to "justice." Jewish tradition often affirms the Lord's commitment to *dikaiosyne*.

What exactly is considered "righteous" behavior depends on the context, the people involved, and the implicit or explicit standard of right and wrong. Sometimes this can get complicated. For instance, if you lie to protect a friend you might be considered having done "right" by your friend, while doing "wrong" by your wider community's commitment to honesty. In early Hellenistic Jewish writings, "righteousness" takes for granted that the God of Israel is the one who determines what is right, and the focus is on the covenant community. The Law of Israel is the written standard of righteous behavior. But ultimately Jewish righteousness is conceived relationally—thinking and doing rightly toward God and toward fellow Jews.

Jews in this period commonly referred to the covenant people as "the righteous," not because they always did the right thing but due to their privileged status in the covenant and their possession of the holy Law that directed them in the righteous ways of God (LXX Ps 36:29; Eccl 3:16; Prov 24:15). But at the same time the biblical tradition recognized the sinfulness of Israel and the reality of waywardness and disobedience to the covenant.

For instance, the prophet Daniel confesses the sins of Israel on behalf of the people. The following is a translation of the Septuagint text:

Righteousness [*dikaiosynē*] belongs to you, O Lord, and
the shame of our face belongs to us, on this day, to the
people of Judah and the settlers in Jerusalem and to all the

people of Israel . . . because of the trespasses that they have
perpetrated before you. O Master, the shame of our face
belongs to us and to our kings and sovereigns and to our
ancestors, because we have sinned against you. To the Lord
belongs justice [*dikaiosynē*] and mercy, for we have rebelled
against you and have not obeyed the voice of the Lord our
God by following your law, which you gave before Moses
and us through your servants the prophets. (Dan 9:7–10
NETS, slightly modified)

Israel wrestled with the paradox of being holy to God and
righteous by virtue of being God's special people, while at
the same time needing to live in accordance with the specific
religious and moral standards outlined in the Law. In fact, in
Galatians Paul alludes to Psalm 143:2 along these lines:

No one will be justified by the works of the law. (Gal 2:16)

> Do not enter into judgment with your servant,
>   for no one living is righteous before you.
>   (Ps 143:2)

Paul uses the Greek verb *dikaioō* here, and the exact
meaning and proper translation of this term (derived from
dikaios) is a matter of debate in scholarship.

Dikaioō, the verbal form of *dikaios*, has a range of mean-
ings in the Septuagint, and this is instructive and informative
for thinking through Paul's usage. The primary orientation
for the meaning of *dikaioō* is the recognition or conferral of
righteousness from a judge or authority (LXX Deut 25:1;
2 Sam 15:4). A good example is 1 Kings 8:32, which recognizes that God will hear from heaven and judge his people;
an unrighteous person will be deemed by God to be a

lawbreaker, and a righteous person will be declared just. Put
simply, the righteous person can count on God to make his
judicial pronouncement in accordance with the person's true
righteousness. That *pronouncement* is God's "justifying" of the
person (*dikaioō*). A judge or authority *recognizes* the righteousness of a just person.

Where this gets complicated is the fact that God is not
just committed to judging Israel, but also protecting Israel.
So, sometimes the verb *dikaioō* is used not just for the recognition of "rightness" but for seeking or defending justice:

> Give justice to orphan and poor;
> of lowly and needy maintain the right [*dikaioō*].
> (LXX Psalm 81:3)

> Defend the orphan,
> And do justice [*dikaioō*] to the widow.
> (LXX Isa 1:17)

In both of these cases, God's covenant commitment to
doing right by Israel means that he will defend or secure
the well-being of the needy, the lowly, and the widow. This
is more than making a declaration in a courtroom; it is the
"rightwising" work of the almighty God who is determined
to make good on his promises to Israel. We learn from the
Septuagint's usage of *dikaioō* that this verb reflects God's
commitment to righteousness. He doesn't *make* anything
"righteous" in an artificial way. *Dikaioō* reflects God's innate
desire for everything to conform to his standard of righteousness and justice.

Sometimes *dikaioō* is used for humans who are seeking to
"justify" themselves. A couple of examples in the Gospel of
Luke are worth noting:

But wanting to justify [*dikaioō*] himself, he asked Jesus, "And who is my neighbor?" (Luke 10:29)

So he said to them, "You are those who justify [*dikaioō*] yourselves in the sight of others; but God knows your hearts; for what is prized by human beings is an abomination in the sight of God. (Luke 16:15)[1]

In both of these texts, a human is wanting to demonstrate his own right behavior in accordance with a certain standard. In the first text, the man wants to defend his righteousness with respect to keeping the covenantal command to love one's neighbor. In the second text, Jesus is accusing the Pharisees of wanting only to be in the good graces of the populace, thus running the risk of disregarding what God wants. They want to be proven "right" in the eyes of peers and whom they consider to be important people.

RIGHTEOUSNESS AND JUSTIFICATION LANGUAGE IN PAUL

Now, it is time to look at how Paul uses the language of righteousness and justification. We will save Galatians for the next section. Here our goal is to get a sweeping understanding of how Paul engages with *dikaios* terminology.

The first thing to say is that Paul believed God is righteous and cares about a just world (Rom 2:5). However, because of sin, people have become wicked (Rom 3:10). The gospel of Jesus Christ is meant to address two problems—human alienation from and enmity with God, and human sinfulness and unrighteousness. Both of these elements are addressed

---

1. According to Luke, Jesus made this statement to certain Pharisees who were critical of his teaching.

by the gospel according to Paul. In Romans, Paul famously describes the gospel as the revelation of the "righteousness of God" (Rom 1:17). Scholars have strongly disagreed over this phrase (*diakiosynē theou*) throughout the years. Is it a status transferred from the righteous God to sinful mortals? Is it an event—God's righteous activity for the salvation of sinners? Or, is it an attribute of God, his eternal commitment to justice? I think the most natural way to take the phrase is as a moral attribute, but this attribute is on full display in the activity of the gospel. Through Jesus Christ, God has initiated a major step of his plan to make all things right, which begins with reconciling sinners to himself by faith (Rom 3:21, 30). Jesus is the one mediator to establish this reconciliation: he is righteousness in himself, becoming the perfectly righteous human being not tainted by sin and thereby establishing a new pattern of righteousness for humans as they conform to his image (1 Cor 1:30; 6:11).

The mechanism for obtaining this righteousness is faith. Paul is insistent that justification happens by faith alone, and not by works of the Law (Rom 4:5, 22; 10:10). This faith is a covenantal dynamic of trust, just as Abraham believed God and it was reckoned as "righteousness" (Rom 4:3). Such a faith is not a cognitive phenomenon of maintaining a mental checklist of "beliefs"; it is an active engagement of trust and hope in God. Faith itself is not saving, just as "taking medicine" doesn't cure a disease. The medicine itself cures, but taking the medicine is the means of getting the cure to the right place.

Paul presents the "right-making" work of God in the gospel of Jesus Christ as the conferral of a new status ("righteous"), but also as more than that—as a transformation through the Spirit and through Jesus Christ: "For our sake he made him to be sin who knew no sin, so that in him we might become the righteousness of God" (2 Cor 5:21). As Christ took on the human burden of living the sinner's life and paying the sinner's penalty (though he himself was without sin), so believers are granted the privilege of sharing in what Christ is, the "righteousness of God" (*dikaiosynē theou*). This appears to mean more than just having a status of "righteous." As believers are united with Christ, they are conformed to his righteous being, becoming more and more righteous as a result of that transformative participation. This may help explain what Paul means when he tells the Romans that Christ was "raised for our justification" (Rom 4:25): in his resurrected human body, the Lord Jesus Christ has created the ultimate form of the righteous human, providing a model for believers.

A key message we learn from the range of Paul's use of righteousness/justification language is that he was interested in more than just believers obtaining a status of "justification" before God. While reconciling with God is the heart of the gospel of Jesus Christ, a real standard of moral righteousness is still important to New Creation. Paul clarifies that it is not just the *hearers* of the Law who are righteous, but the *doers* (Rom 2:13). After all, "the kingdom of God is not food and drink but *righteousness* and peace and joy in the Holy Spirit" (Rom 14:17). If the kingdom is all about righteousness, how can sinners be "fit" for the kingdom if they do not become righteous?

JUSTIFICATION IN GALATIANS

As we turn to Galatians, Paul does not engage with as wide a range of teaching on *dikaiosynē* as we see in Romans. That is because he was addressing a specific issue in relationship to justification and covenant belonging in conversation with the Galatians and the instruction of third-party teachers.

The key matter seems to be the question of how gentiles become "right" with God, i.e., enter the covenantal family of the God of Israel. It appears that the rival teachers (who were correcting or supplementing Paul's teaching after he had left Galatia) were trying to convince the gentile Galatian believers that they could only truly enter the Messiah's family and be "justified" by adhering to the covenantal Law, the Law of Moses. This was not about earning God's favor. Jews, as we noted earlier, already knew that they were spoiled by sin and were unrighteous before God. They relied on God's graciousness and mercy. But these teachers were advocating that the gentile believers find their place in God's family through circumcision and keeping the Law, doing as Israel had long done since Moses. Now, I don't think these rival teachers did *not* teach the importance of "faith." They would have known Habakkuk 2:4 teaches that the righteous live by faith. What I do imagine these other teachers had in mind is that being justified before God happens through the Messiah (Jesus) and is "by faith" in the Messiah, but the means of expressing that faith is obeying the "works of the Law." This was not legalism versus faith. This was faith expressed in a certain set of works: the works of the Law.

Paul saw it differently, because the Law privileges Jews but the ultimate vision for God's great big family is that all are welcome and treated on equal terms, Jew and gentile, slave and free, male and female. A person is justified by faith in Jesus Christ alone (2:16–17). Anything that is "required" above and beyond this becomes a requirement for justification, which then takes away from the death of Christ (2:21).

Paul takes the focus off of Moses and puts it on Abraham. Abraham was not counted as righteous before God because of certain works, but because he *believed* God (3:6); essentially, he was justified "by faith." And because God gave to Abraham the promise of the blessing of the nations, the gentiles can look to Abraham as the great progenitor, the model of justification by faith (Gal 3:8).

Paul was aware that his reasoning could come across as antagonistic toward the Law. So, he clarified that the Abrahamic promise (of the blessing of gentiles by faith) does not stand in opposition to the Law. The Law was never meant to be a rival means for justification (3:21), but played a crucial yet temporary role of guarding and holding Israel in custody until the time of Christ, so that at last believers could be justified by faith (3:24). The Law could make the people of Israel aware of sin and discipline them to ensure their own final good. However, justification and transformation toward righteousness would require the messianic leadership of Jesus and the sanctifying work of the Spirit (5:4–6).

ONGOING QUESTIONS IN DEBATE

As conversations continue in Pauline scholarship about justification, there appear to be three key questions. I will dare to give my own brief attempts to answer these in relation to Paul's writings, but I am keenly aware that these are hotly debated matters. I encourage readers to pursue some of the suggested reading to explore other approaches and get into arguments and evidence with more depth.

Is Justification a Vertical Doctrine or a Horizontal Doctrine?

The New Perspective on Paul brought a deeper awareness of social dynamics of inclusion and exclusion in the early churches to the conversation about Pauline theology. Justification has been presented by some as pertaining to the question of who belongs "inside" the covenant community and who belongs "outside." Those who hold to a more

traditional (Reformational) view of justification tend to stand
by the idea that justification is about being counted righteous
before God. Essentially, justification is a vertical doctrine, not
a horizontal one. However, I think that a both–and dynamic
is going on here when we look at Paul's discussions. In its
primary sense, "justification" is about being right with *God*,
but there are also social implications. Just as Jesus criticized
some of the Pharisees for seeking to be *justified* in the eyes of
mortals (rather than God), there are complex dynamics at
play in the biblical language of righteousness. Justification is
indeed about the sinner and God, but that relationship takes
place within communities.

Is Justification a Status of Righteousness or a Reality of Righteousness?

We have argued that the verb *dikaioō* tends to be used with
reference to a declaration of being "right" with God. That
status is important. Abraham believed, and *that* was treated
as righteousness. When sinners confess their sin and believe
in Jesus Christ, they are "justified." They, like Abraham, are
justified before God. But it is not enough to leave justification
there as some kind of legal fiction. The transforming work
of God's Spirit and the formative lordship of Christ means
that the believer is *changed*. Paul, after all, explains to the
Romans that the power of Sin and Death is broken by Christ,
so they are no longer slaves to these evil powers. Believers now
have true freedom to follow God and become "instruments
of righteousness." Sin is no longer master, because of the
grace of God (Rom 6:12–14). This relates to Paul's comment
in 2 Corinthians that believers *become* the "righteousness of
God" (5:21). There is a kind of gravitational pull toward righteousness; wherever the Spirit resides, the believer's life will
be formed toward the just and right ways of God.

Is Justification Provisional or Final?

Scholars continue to wrestle with the two affirmations Paul makes about (1) the grace of justification by faith and (2) the reality of judgment according to works (Rom 2:6; 2 Cor 5:10). How do these relate? Is justification "provisional," a kind of free pass until judgment? Or is it final, the righteous status of Christ which supersedes or cancels out final judgment according to works? If the latter, then why does Paul mention a real day of reckoning for believers as something they need to prepare for (1 Thess 3:11–13; 5:23–24; Rom 2:16; 15:16)? There are no easy answers to this. Somehow, both are true. The grace of God is powerful, and the justifying work of Christ has no limitations or vulnerabilities. God saves sinners; they don't save themselves. But there must be some form of "cooperation" involved (Phil 2:12–13; 1 Cor 15:10). Yes, the believer receives God's forgiveness and justification by faith alone, but there still must be an active participation in the work of the Spirit to bear the fruit of righteousness that God cares about. In the end, believers are not judged on the deeds they have performed out of their own human strength apart from God. Rather, the final judgment and the evaluation of human deeds will reflect a life lived in surrender and devotion to God.

FURTHER READING

Beilby, James K., and Paul Rhodes Eddy, eds. *Justification: Five Views.* Downers Grove: IVP Academic, 2011.

Bird, Michael F. *Introducing Paul: The Man, His Mission, and His Message.* Downers Grove: IVP Academic, 2008.

————. *The Saving Righteousness of God: Studies on Paul, Justification and the New Perspective.* Eugene, OR: Wipf & Stock, 2007.

Byrne, Brendan. *Paul and the Economy of Salvation: Reading from the Perspective of the Last Judgment.* Grand Rapids: Baker Academic, 2021.

Gorman, Michael J. *Inhabiting the Cruciform God: Kenosis, Justification, and Theosis in Paul's Narrative Soteriology.* Grand Rapids: Eerdmans, 2009.

Stanley, Alan P., and Robert N. Wilkin, eds. *Four Views on the Role of Works at the Final Judgment.* Grand Rapids: Zondervan, 2013.

Westerholm, Stephen. *Justification Reconsidered: Rethinking a Pauline Theme.* Grand Rapids: Eerdmans, 2013.

Wright, N. T. *Justification: God's Plan & Paul's Vision.* Downers Grove: IVP Academic, 2009.

Yinger, Kent L. *Paul, Judaism, and Judgment according to Deeds.* SNTSMS. Cambridge: Cambridge University Press, 1999.

Subject Index

Abraham
  blessing of, 18, 19, 20, 48, 51,
    63–65, 75, 90, 99, 136–37
  and faith, 77, 81, 88–93, 96–97,
    99, 134, 136, 138
  as forefather of Israel, 63, 63n. 8
  justified by works as well as
    faith, 81
  as prototype of true believer,
    64, 90–91, 99, 137
  two sons of, 22, 65, 106–7
adoption, 66–67, 69
Antiochus IV, 109
Apostles' Creed, the, 76
Aristotle, 113–14

baptism, 69
Barnabas, 15, 16, 17, 106, 118
believing community, the. *See*
  family of God, the

Cephas (Peter), 15, 16–17, 37, 85
Christianity, as creedal religion,
  76
church, the. *See* family of God,
  the
Cicero, 116–17
circumcision

act itself as neither good nor
  bad, 4, 5, 30–31, 37, 65,
  101, 118
false teaching of as necessary
  for Gentiles, 4–5, 7, 10, 16,
  22–23, 30–31, 37, 84–85,
  89, 117
as mark of Jews as Jews, 10
as mark of righteousness, 5, 8,
  42, 89–90, 92
as symbol of Galatians cutting
  themselves off from
  Christ, 4–5, 7–8, 23, 37,
  42, 65, 108, 117–19
as unnecessary for Gentiles, 10,
  15–16, 22, 25, 47, 64, 84,
  106, 117–19
cooperation, 72

David, King, 60
devotion, 101–2

Epictetus, 114–15, 116
Euripides, 114

faith
  Abraham and, 77, 81, 88–93,
    96–97, 99, 134, 136, 138

as anti-reason, 78–79
call of Jesus for, 76
of Christ, 86–88, 86n. 7, 86n. 8
covenantal, 77, 94–95, 96, 134
as doctrine, 78
emphasis on in Christianity, 76
era of, 97–100
as faithfulness, 100–102
and freedom from the Law, 97,
    99–100
household of, 102
human agency in, 40–41
justification by, 4, 9, 16-20,
    26, 39, 43, 47, 63, 80–86,
    88–94, 99–100, 134, 136,
    139
language of, 76–77, 78, 79–80,
    83, 86–88, 101
misleading assumptions about,
    77–79, 80
as passive, 77–78, 80
righteousness through, 5, 64, 81,
    88–89, 92–97, 134-35, 138
tie that binds family of God
    together, 58
true, 1, 9, 13–14, 17, 23, 42,
    76, 92
vs. works, 9, 16–17, 19, 43, 48,
    64, 77–78, 80–86, 88–93,
    95, 97, 134, 136
working through love, 78, 101
family
  church, the, as a, 50, 102
  importance of in ancient
    world, 50, 55–56
  language of in Galatians,
    55–58, 74
  See also family of God
family of God
  all welcome in, 18, 48, 57, 73,
    136

believing community as, 50,
    55, 57
brothers and sisters in, 56,
    69–75
equality of all members of,
    50–51, 55, 57, 64, 68–69,
    73, 75, 136
father and son in, 57, 58–62
faith in Jesus as doorway into,
    39, 48, 55, 62, 63–65,
    66–69, 71, 74–75, 100, 102
generosity in, 51, 52
guided by love in relations with
    one another, 74
humility in, 52
as incorporated into the sonship
    of Jesus, 68–69
lack of competition in, 50, 72, 73
personal responsibility in, 51–52
flesh, the
  freedom and, 123–25
  Ishmael as symbol of, 65
  language of in Galatians,
    123–25
  living by, 24–25, 24n. 14, 55,
    100–101, 123–25
  vs. the spirit, 24n. 14, 25,
    100–101, 117, 123–25
  works of, 100, 124
freedom
  in Christ, 5, 7, 22–23, 41, 54,
    71, 104, 105, 111–13, 138
  and the flesh, 117, 123–25
  as flourishing in the family of
    God, 58
  in Greco-Roman philosophical
    discourse, 113–17
  from the Law, through faith,
    97, 98–99, 104, 117–23, 125
  Isaac as symbol of God's, 22, 65
  Israel's journey to, 108–9

Paul's conception of, 32, 35–36
presence of in letter to the
    Galatians, 35–36, 35n. 10
role of in redemption, 35, 137
as super-entity, 36
huiothesia, 67
humility, 52, 63

Isaac, 22, 65, 107, 108
Ishmael, 22, 65, 108
Israel, sonship of, 60

Jesus
    as agent of salvation, 32, 33, 39,
      40, 99
    call to faith of, 76
    came to free people from the
      Law, 8, 20–21, 22–23,
      97–99
    communion of with God, 60,
      62
    faith in as doorway into the
      Father's family, 39, 48,
      55, 62, 63–65, 66–69, 71,
      74–75, 100, 102
    as mediator between God and
      his people, 88, 134
    participating in, 33–35, 41–42,
      69, 74–75
    Paul's conception of, 32, 33
    as primary agent in letter to
      the Galatians, 33–35
    as proxy of God's activity, 33,
      33n. 4
    pure sufficiency of, 4, 38, 119
    righteousness of, 54, 134–35,
      139
    sent by the Father, 62, 62n. 7
    as Son of God, 32, 33, 55, 56,
      59–60, 61, 62, 68, 73
Judaism, Paul within, 48–49

justification
    and becoming right with God,
      39–41, 58, 62–63, 90, 93,
      99, 136, 138
    by faith, 4, 9, 16-20, 26, 39,
      43, 47, 63, 80–86, 88–94,
      99–100, 134, 136, 139
    in Galatians, 135–37
    Paul's language of, 39, 129–35
    provisional vs. final, 139
    vertical vs. horizontal, 137–38
    by works, 4, 7, 9, 17, 18, 39, 43,
      63, 80–86, 93–94, 119,
      134, 136

Law, the
    adherence to as unnecessary
      for Gentiles, 15, 19, 22, 47,
      48, 64, 84, 106, 117–19
    apocalyptic Paul approach to,
      11, 40–41
    approaches to in Paul's
      thought, 8–13
    as confinement, 119–21
    era of, 97, 98–99
    freedom and, 117–23, 125
    as identity badge, 46–47
    Jesus freeing people from, 8,
      20–21, 22–23, 85–86, 97–99
    limitations of, 19–20, 44–45,
      69, 97–98, 120–21, 122, 137
    new perspective approach to,
      9–11, 13, 39n. 16, 46–48
    as *paidagogos*, 12, 45, 48, 98,
      121–23
    Reformation approach to, 9
    as reigning in transgressions, 44,
      45, 97–98, 99, 120–21, 137
    reliance on brings a curse, 8, 18
    righteousness through, 44, 119,
      130, 135

Scripture Index